LEWIS B. SMEDES

WHAT IT
TAKES TO LIVE
WITH COURAGE,

HONESTY,

AND

GRATITUDE

A Life *of* Distinction

SHAW BOOKS

an imprint of WaterBrook Press

A Life of Distinction
A SHAW BOOK
PUBLISHED BY WATERBROOK PRESS
2375 Telstar Drive, Suite 160
Colorado Springs, Colorado 80920
A division of Random House, Inc.

ISBN 0-87788-607-5

Library of Congress Cataloging-in-Publication Data
Smedes, Lewis B.
  A life of distinction : what it takes to live with courage, honesty, and gratitude /
Lewis B. Smedes
    p. cm.
  ISBN 0-87788-607-5
  1. Conduct of life. 2. Smedes, Lewis B. 3. Christian life. I. Title.
BJ1581.2 S522 2002
170'.44—dc21   2001055139

Printed in the United States of America
2002

10 9 8 7 6 5 4 3 2 1

To my friends
Els and Sandor Ungvari

Nobilitas Probata Florescit

CONTENTS

ACKNOWLEDGMENTS

I am grateful for some pretty good people who have walked my way and become my very good friends. From their friendship, more than from anything else, I have learned what pretty good people are like. The reader will find a few of them in this book. To two of them, I dedicated it. But there are many more. And I wish I knew how to thank them for being my friends.

There are some scholars who helped me too. Professor James Gustafson first helped me see how important discernment is on the journey to goodness. Professor Gilbert Meilander got me to think about gratitude. Dr. Robert Coles—in his book *The Morality of Children*—opened my eyes to the courage of people like Ruby Bridges. Professor Stanley Hauerwas, who has been writing profoundly about moral character for a long time, goaded me to do some thinking about it on my own, and in my own way. And, then, of course, there is always Aristotle. The seed for "Fopke's Dream" was sown in my head a long time ago by Fyodor Dostoyevsky. Saint Paul is in a class by himself.

I am thankful for a few friends who helped me by reading my manuscript fairly early on. I must mention Elaine and Donald Postema and Doris Smedes especially. But thanks, too, to Clifford Penner, Mary Rotzien, and Carol Visser.

As always, *Soli Deo Gloria*.

The Sort of Person Everybody Wants to Be

Deep in every healthy person's heart simmers a longing to live a life of distinction. To be a good person. A *pretty* good person, at least. Every now and then we sense a fine urge inside of us that leaves us unsatisfied with what we are. And, for a moment fled too soon, we feel the flutter of a longing always to be the person we were in that fleeting encounter with our truest self.

If you think you might be an exception, I want to ask you a simple question: How do you want people to remember you after you die? I mean people who matter to you. Maybe your children. People who know the sort of person you really are. Think about it. How do you want them to remember you? How we want to be remembered is a sure sign of the sort of person we really want to be.

We do not easily get rid of the urge to be a good person. It survives all the other seductions. It even outlasts the three restless desires of every modern heart—the urge to *feel* good, the urge to *make* good, and the urge to *look* good.

Feeling good! Feeling satisfied, feeling fulfilled,

feeling free, feeling warm, feeling loved, feeling anything at all so long as it satisfies our consuming hunger
for pleasure-giving feelings. Our commitment to pleas-
ant feelings is like a religious devotion; its sacred relics
are the Valium bottle, the wine goblet, and the self-
help book; Woodstock was its Pentecost, anybody's
favorite therapist its high priest.

Then there is *looking* good! Looking sharp, being
in shape, a well-toned body draped in designer clothes
and topped with an attractive face. Making a good
impression, turning people's heads, listening for the
ultimate benediction: "You look fantastic." Looking
good—the blessed vision of the cult of appearances.
Jane Fonda is one of its sacred symbols, and the health
spa its wayside chapel.

And, of course, *making* good! To make something
of ourselves, get a little power, make a modest mint of
money, and be well known for at least a day. Making it
big—the heavenly hope of the religion of success. The
hot investment counselor is its prophet, and the stock
exchange its high altar.

The sacred trinity of *feeling* good, *looking* good, and
making good are very good goods, but they make very
bad gods. As gods they eventually leave us feeling like
spent dreams on the soiled sheets of disenchantment.
But plant them in the good of *being* good, and we may
have what it takes to make a fine life for ourselves.

So it is time we face up to the sort of people we
want to be inside the people we appear to be, to look

to our better dreams, our nobler inclinations, the set of our soul's mainsails, or, in Alexis de Tocqueville's fetching phrase, the "habits of our hearts." Time to wonder what it would be like to be a pretty good person in a pretty spoiled world.

Pretty good people still sweat it out against some wild, and some mild, corruptions that inhabit their frail spirits. The best people I know are muddling their way through a mess of moral rubbish on the steep road to character. Good and bad crisscross through their circuits continually, thumbing their noses at each other as they pass. Sometimes the good signal is louder. Sometimes the bad. But the odds are better than ever that they will hear the good signals most of the time.

Why has the possibility of *being* a pretty good person lately recaptured our imagination? I think there are at least two reasons.

The first reason is this: We have discovered that personal goodness is a positive and attractive power. For too long "good people" were doormats who never hurt anybody, never complained, and always caved in to what other people asked. Actually the good people are the strong ones. They are the people with guts who are in charge of their own lives, who weave all their colorful selves together in a seamless garment of personal wholeness. And they are the people who know how to love a person with a love that builds and a love that lasts. Good people are complicated people, rich tapestries, endlessly interesting, yet simple and clear. In short, we have found out that good people are more exciting than bad people.

The second reason we are rediscovering "good" is our hunch that something bad happens to all of us when people go bad on us. Big-time brokers cheat on the system and defraud the people who trusted it. Rich and powerful people betray the trust of little people. Preachers of the gospel cheat their followers out of cash and hang out in scruffy brothels. Political leaders violate the rules of their own game. And while the haves are stuffing their pockets with more, people living all around them have no homes and their children do not have enough to eat. It makes us wonder: What sort of people are we getting to be?

The quick response to moral breakdown is to appoint committees to make new codes to guide our ethics. But we do not fail because we lack codes. We fail because we lack character.

This book deals only in fundamentals, the raw materials, meat and potatoes from start to finish—the basic makings of a pretty good person. Not the supernatural stuff you need for sainthood, but the common qualities of humanity. Things like gratitude, guts, simple integrity, self-control, discernment, and fair love.

These are the makings. But I want you to see them come alive in the real people you will meet in these pages. People on the way to goodness, some of them on the edge of greatness, most of them just pretty good human beings trying to beat the odds: real people. Here and there, more often than you expect, you will discover images of yourself: the self you really want to be, maybe the self you are, certainly the self you were meant to be.

CHAPTER 1

A Little Gratitude

Doris huffed back into our apartment on a frightfully cold December morning and found me collapsed on the tiled kitchen floor. My face, she told me later, was a dirty gray, eyes open but looking nowhere, conveying to her a sure sense of death. She kept her head, checked my pulse, and listened for some breathing. When she was satisfied that I had enough breath in me to last a few minutes, she rushed out to call an ambulance. The driver hooked me up to an oxygen tank, loaded us both aboard, and skidded us down a country road into the trauma center of the hospital that serves the sturdy people of St. Cloud, Minnesota.

We had pushed each other out of bed early, even though it was thirty degrees below zero outside, because we were planning to pack our things to leave Minnesota that day and get moving back to our house in Sierra Madre, California. Doris and I had been living at St. John's University, a stone's throw from St. Cloud, for a few months' sabbatical and were primed for taking off. I had slept poorly, bothered by dull aches in my right calf during the night, and I got up from bed with a feeling of unease about myself. But, it being traveling day, I tried to ignore it.

We pulled some clothes over our thermal-knit underwear, ate bowls of hot oatmeal, drank cups of black coffee, and tuned to public radio for late reports on road conditions to the south of us, where it had been snowing heavily for several days. My unsteadiness did not go away, so I decided to curl up on the couch for a few minutes before I got serious about packing.

Doris told me that she was going out to get some traveling suggestions from Sister Delores, a lanky, handsome woman and the resident specialist on managing Minnesota roads in winter. But actually, with her intuition for things that might be going wrong, she went to ask for the name of a doctor she might call just in case I was really ill. Having gotten one, she walked back into the kitchen and found me lying near the telephone that had called me off the couch, looking quite dead.

My lungs, it turned out, had been spattered by a buckshot of blood clots, and for a couple of days at the hospital I tilted heavily in death's direction. On the fourth day a benign Norwegian physician by the name of Hans Engman leaned over my bed and congratulated me on surviving the twenty-to-one odds that medical statistics had stacked up against me.

"Oh yeah? That's terrific, doctor."

My heart was not awash with gratitude—mostly, I suppose, because until he told me that I was going to live, I had not thought at all of dying. I closed my eyes and went back to sleep.

A couple of nights later—in the moody hush that settles on a hospital room at two o'clock in the morning, alone, with no drugs inside of me to set me up for it—I was seized with a frenzy of gratitude. Possessed! My arms rose straight up by themselves, a hundred-pound weight could not have held them at my side. My hands open, my fingers spread, waving, twisting, while I blessed the Lord above for the almost unbearable goodness of being alive on this good earth in this good body at this present time.

I was flying outside of myself, high, held in weightless lightness, as if my earthly existence needed no ground to rest in, but was hung in space with only love to keep it aloft.

It was then I learned that gratitude is the best feeling I would ever have, the ultimate joy of living. It was better than sex, better than winning a lottery, better than watching your daughter graduate from college, better and deeper than any other feeling; it is, perhaps, the genesis of all other really good feelings in the human repertoire. I am sure that nothing in life can ever match the feeling of being held in being by a gracious energy percolating from the abyss where beats the loving heart of God.

AN OPPORTUNITY OF A LIFETIME

Gratitude is our gladness. We were born to it.

Inside the itchy hankering of every heart stirs an aching need to feel grateful. We are heavy until we feel the lightness of gratitude. We hear the sweet music of joy only when we feel some awe and wonder and delight, and surprise, too, at being our own best gift. But once we have felt it, we know that there is no pleasure on earth like it.

My mother had a heavier way with gratitude. Whenever I groused about my lot in life, she whacked my conscience with this solemn bromide: "Lewis, you ought to be grateful." She was right, I suppose, to press gratitude into the mold of duty: we *ought* to be grateful.

Are we not butterflies fluttering on the fragile flower of existence, sipping life freely from God's own nectaries? And ought we not to be grateful for the privilege?

Mother only echoed the wisdom of all ages. The Roman sage Cicero called it the "mother of all virtue." And listen to the ancient stoic Seneca: "There was never any man so wicked as not to approve of gratitude and detest ingratitude."

The apostle Paul told us that most of the malignancies that cramp the human spirit slither out of a swamp of ingratitude: "For although they knew God... they neither glorified him as God nor gave thanks to him" (Romans 1:21). Which, I suppose, makes ingratitude a prime candidate for the original sin. The premier theologian of our own age, Karl Barth, said that gratitude is "the one thing which is unconditionally and inescapably demanded" of us.

Immanuel Kant, the father of modern philosophy, agreed in his own way: "Ingratitude," he wrote, "is the essence of vileness." And Shakespeare's Viola, of *Twelfth Night,* felt it like moral nausea in her own heart:

> I hate ingratitude more in a man than lying, vainness, babbling drunkenness, or any taint of vice whose strong corruption inhabits our frail blood.

Settled! Ingratitude reeks. It decays the spirit, spoils the soul, and decomposes life itself into a fetid swamp. It is the lie that fundamentally falsifies the essence of living. So we ought to be grateful.

Still, I wonder whether it does much good to say so. I know I ought to be grateful, but I also know that it does not help me much to know it. I have a hunch that nobody ever actually *feels* grateful out of a sense of obligation. Of course anybody can fumble through the civil courtesies. But do we *feel* grateful on command?

On one Thanksgiving Day, a long time ago, I learned that it does not do me much good to know I ought to be grateful. That was the year my mother told us that we could not afford a chicken for Thanksgiving dinner; we would have a nice pot roast instead. Fowl came dear in those days—a dressed broiler could cost a couple of dollars, while for fifty or sixty cents you could get a pot roast without too much fat in it big enough for a family of six.

I took it poorly. It was a matter of status with me. I knew that Clary Kramer and Bud Bishop were going to brag to me about how much they had eaten on Thanksgiving Day, and they would ask me how much chicken I had eaten, and I would have to say that we had eaten pot roast.

"Pot roast? On Thanksgiving Day? What kind of nutty family have you got?"

In our neighborhood, if a kid's mother was too poor to buy a holiday chicken, his status was under a cloud. So what does he do? He snivels. He whines. He makes his mother feel sorry for him.

The afternoon before Thanksgiving Day, moving on toward five o'clock, my mother put on her coat, trudged a half-mile to Hans Helling's butcher shop, and bought us a fat hen. It was almost the last one, hanging by the neck from one of a row of hooks where butchers strung up their fresh meat while it dripped blood on the sawdust floor. She brought it home, laid it limp on the kitchen table, and said, "There, we're going to have chicken tomorrow."

Catherine, my serious-minded older sister, turned on me: "See what you went and made her do? I hope you are grateful." By which she meant: "I hope you feel rotten."

I did feel rotten. But I did not feel much gratitude. What I felt was guilt. Only guilt, deep purple guilt, heavy guilt, for twisting my mother around my wretched whimpers. No joy came to me with Hans Helling's hen. It did me no good at all to know that I was duty bound to be grateful.

And yet every intuition tells me my mother was

right when, for the five hundred and thirty-sixth time, she said: "Lewis, you *ought* to be grateful for what you've got." Life is out of joint whenever a person is ungrateful for its gifts. The beauty of it gets twisted when our spirits do not rejoice and give thanks.

How can we put these two things together, the sure intuition that we have a duty to be grateful and the experience that duty seldom moves us an inch toward the joy of it? The secret lies in the difference between an ought of obligation and an ought of opportunity. "You ought to tell the truth on your income tax report"—there's an ought of obligation for you. "You ought to take advantage of this tax deduction"—here's an ought of opportunity.

We ought to be grateful the way we ought to applaud a great musician who has just set our hearts afire, the way we ought to laugh at a very funny joke, and the way we ought to hug someone we love. We ought to be grateful the way a groom ought to be happy on his wedding day, or a new mother ought to be glad to give her baby suck. Life calls us to gratitude the way the sun says to the buried seed: "You ought to break out of your shell and come alive as the lovely flower you were always meant to be."

Giving and gratitude go together like humor and laughter, like having one's back rubbed and the sigh that follows, like a blowing wind and the murmur of wind chimes. Gratitude keeps alive the rhythm of grace given and grace grateful, a lively lilt that lightens a heavy world.

A GIFT WITH A PERSON ATTACHED

Not everything we get for nothing is a gift. We can be bought with things we get for nothing, and when somebody buys us with something disguised as a gift we are not grateful.

Gratitude happens only when we get a real gift, so it helps if we know a gift when we get one.

Here is a barefooted fellow walking alone on a lonely beach. He steps on something sharp; it pricks him at the tender tendon that ties the big toe to the ball of the foot. He roars, he cusses, he bends over to check his toe for blood, he gropes for whatever it was that stuck him, and—he grabs hold of a diamond brooch.

Finders keepers. Something for nothing. But not a gift.

A crazy millionaire throws a wad of hundred-dollar bills out of a tenth-floor window, letting them flutter like green leaves to the street below. They fall into the fingers of whoever happens to be walking down Tenth Avenue at that moment, shocked into instant greed at the sight of money from heaven. He stretches his neck over the ledge and chortles at the insects hustling for the crumbs he has tossed them.

A bonanza for people down on their luck. But not a gift.

A real gift comes with a giver attached.

Doris and I came home the other night and found a United Parcel Service package on the porch. We opened it. Inside was a white knit afghan, long enough to cover my long body on any davenport. It was a gift from Sue Van Lenten. She had pinned a note to it: "Every inch stitched with love."

Sue Van Lenten is a red-haired beauty who belonged to a parish that I served some forty years ago, nestled in an industrial ghetto of Paterson, New Jersey. For three decades she has kept on caring about us while we lived apart one from the other. So when she set herself to knit us an afghan, she stitched something of herself into her gift. And when we took her gift, we gladly, gratefully took her with it and burrowed ourselves a little deeper into her life.

The charm of a gift with a giver attached is that our thanks has a person attached too. To give thanks is to give one's self to the giver who came tucked into her gift. Gratitude is our way of welcoming the giver, and thanks is our way of stitching an inch of ourselves alongside of her.

A gift without a giver attached is a false thing. It is not really a gift at all; it is just something for nothing, and it does not move us to gratitude. An impersonal gift may be no more than a lure. We know what salespeople are up to when they remember us at Christmas with a bottle of expensive perfume. We know what lobbyists are up to when they offer a Congress member a free vacation in Hawaii. Some people give gifts to people the way a fisherman offers a fly to a trout. We know what's going on; we've just gotten so used to the charade that we don't get upset by it.

But we never feel the gladness of gratitude when we get one of those "gifts."

Having said this much about the sort of gift we are grateful for, I will pass on a few more signs that tell us when something we get for nothing is a real gift.

A Real Gift Costs Something to Give but Nothing to Get

The trash collector finds something worth keeping in a Beverly Hills garbage can, but he does not feel grateful to the rich folk who threw it out. Nor does an underpaid typist feel grateful to a wealthy corporation for handing her a trifling bonus at Christmas time. For something to count as a gift, the person who gives it has to sacrifice something—time, money, talent—it doesn't matter what, or how much, as long as it costs the giver something to give it.

But it costs only to give it. It never costs us anything to receive a real gift.

Where I came from, if someone did you a favor, you would probably say, "Much obliged." These days, when somebody does something for you—puts in a good word for you higher up, buys your lunch, covers for you while you take a breather—you might say, "Thanks, I owe you one." It comes to the same thing: we feel as if the favor puts us in debt to the giver.

Something odd about that. If a gift leaves you a debtor, what you have gotten is a loan, not a real gift. The wisest of men have been blind to this obvious fact. Aristotle said that the superior person doesn't accept too many gifts, because if people give us things they get the advantage over us. Immanuel Kant said that anyone who gives him a gift "has stolen a march on me, and if I do him a favor I am only returning *quid pro quo;* I shall always owe him a debt of gratitude." And, he added, no self-respecting person wants to be caught owing somebody a debt of gratitude.

All I can say to this is that these philosophers were blind to the meaning of gratitude. And if we listen to them, we turn off the last spigot of joy in life. Real gifts do not put us under obligation. Not even the obligation to be grateful. Otherwise, where's the grace in it? Or the joy?

And yet it feels natural and right to want to give something to somebody who has given something to us. Saying "much obliged" is only our way of saying that we want to celebrate the joy of getting a gift by giving someone else the same experience.

When I feel the joy of receiving a gift, my heart nudges me to join creation's ballet, the airy dance of giving and getting and giving again. Not a value for value received, but a share in the grace of life. Isn't this why we give our gifts—ourselves—to God, creation's Giver? Not to pay a debt (who can get even with Him?). But to join *His* ballet, the dance of grace.

Giving Real Gifts Is a Gamble

When we give something, we lose control. The person we give a gift to may flush our gift down the sewer. Or she may give it to her secretary for Christmas. Maybe she will sell it.

Here is a letter to "Dear Abby" I picked up in a place you would not expect to find it, Gilbert Meilander's scholarly book *The Theory and Practice of Virtue*.

> Dear Abby: Last week my sister-in-law had a garage sale, and right out front was displayed the gift my husband and I had given her last Christmas! It had never been used and was sold for less than half of what we paid for it. My husband said it was hers to do whatever she pleased with and that I was stupid and oversensitive to give it a second thought. What do you think?
> —Signed, Hurt.

> Abby replied: "Dear Hurt: Your husband is right when he says that the gift was hers to do with whatever she pleased."

A true gift leaves the giver exposed. Defenses down. Out of control. The person we give it to may sell it at a garage sale. Or give it to her mail carrier for Christmas. It is always a possibility. But the only kind of gift anybody is ever grateful for is a gift the giver risks giving.

Real Gifts Take Us by Surprise

I know someone who, just before Christmas, buys herself a gift and puts it on layaway. As the holiday gets close, she sends her husband to the store to fetch it. She then tapes a card to it that says, "From your loving husband." This way she always gets what she wants, never has to exchange it for something she would rather have gotten. No risk, no surprise. But she never really gets a gift.

Watch a child reconnoiter the Christmas tree: She stoops over several boxes, picks up a package with her name on it, tests its heft, squeezes it, shakes it gingerly, holds it up to her ear as if it could talk to her and tell her what it is, and then sets it back on the floor in the exact spot where it was before. She aches to know. But what she wants most is to be surprised at the moment she receives it.

Sometimes we are surprised by what we have known all along; the familiar suddenly glows with newness. I have walked down a street five hundred times without noticing a fantastic liquidambar—the only tree that turns a New England color in the Southern California autumn—and then, without expecting it, I see it one day for the beautiful gift it is.

I live for a week feeling stressed and begrudging when suddenly, for no special reason, I am walloped with wonder that I should be alive, here and now, with thoughts in my head, feelings in my heart, visions in my mind. I am possessed by gratitude. A few lines from G. K. Chesterton say it better than I ever could:

> *The mystery of life*
> *is the plainest part of it.*
> *Whatever else we've grown accustomed to,*
> *we have grown accustomed*
> *to the unaccountable.*

Not even a real gift gives a guarantee that we will be grateful for it. The giver does not have magic power. And the receiver cannot turn on gratitude the way she turns on a smile. We have limited control of the attitude of gratitude. All we can do is keep the windows open so that it can get in when it comes near.

GETTING READY FOR IT

Gratitude dances through the open windows of our hearts. We cannot force it. We cannot create it. And we can certainly close our windows to keep it out. But we can also keep them open and be ready for joy when it comes.

We Can Learn to Celebrate Imperfect Gifts

The perfect gift comes only now and then; most gifts are slightly flawed. But if we focus on the flaws, we quench the joy. People who demand perfection of gifts choke gratitude before it gets a chance to make them or anyone else glad.

My own sainted mother was always grateful to God for His good gifts, but she did not encourage us to celebrate the imperfect gifts that we gave to each other. I have told this story before, but I am going to tell it again, because it makes the point better than any other story that I can think of.

I was visiting my oldest sister, Jessie, in Muskegon, Michigan. Jessie had a fine way with a needle and thread. On this particular occasion I noticed that her son was wearing an uncommonly handsome jacket, and I complimented him on it.

"Mother made it."

"Fine work, Jessie. How in the world do you do it?"

"Oh, there's not much of a trick to it after you've made a few. Would you like me to make one for you?"

"Not possible. I'm heading back to California tomorrow."

"No problem. I'll take your measurements now and tell you how much material we need. When you get home you can buy some wool that you like, send it to me, and I'll have the jacket for you next time you come."

Back home, Doris told me that nobody could make a jacket for a man without a fitting—can't get the shoulders right, she said. But she went along to a fabric store with me anyway, and we picked out several yards of tawny camel's hair, wrapped it up, and sent it off.

A few months later I was back in Muskegon on some academic chore, sitting in my mother's parlor on a Sunday afternoon waiting for Jessie. She finally drove up, parked in front of the house, and walked up to the front door. My jacket, looking a little more gold than tawny now, was draped over her arm. My mother poured a cup of tea. "How're the kids?" "Just fine, how're yours?" And we eventually gained courage to face the question: Would the jacket fit?

I put it on. I made a full turn, and took a long look at myself in a mirror. I turned to Jessie: "What do you think?"

"I think it fits fine."

"So do I."

Gloria in Excelsis Deo!

The wonder of a good gift from someone's hands, the ultimate truth of life in a world made whole by giving and gratitude.

And then a voice came from an overstuffed chair in the corner, the voice of a mother who had looked at all sides of the matter, considered them very carefully, and came regretfully to the conclusion that things were not quite perfect.

"I don't like the color."

Joy died. It always dies for people who can be grateful only for perfect gifts.

I escaped a similar bind one afternoon after I had finished reading the galley proofs of a small book I had written. I should tell you that I crawl through a mine-field of self-doubts whenever I sit down to write a page. Who am I to suppose that my thoughts are worth setting on paper, or that anyone else should want to read them, let alone pay good money to buy them? But I had plowed through my doubts and now the book was done.

I read the proofs in a single day. When I came to the end, in spite of all my doubts, I was possessed by a sense that what I had written was, after all, a pretty good book. It was not a great book, it was an imperfect one, to be sure; but it was an honest book, a clear book, a book anyone could read, maybe with some profit and possibly even a little pleasure.

I do not know how a book happens. How does anyone sew a bunch of disconnected thoughts together on the thread of a strong idea? How do stories get into one's head? How does something that happened a long time ago get born again in one's memory? I could not tell how this book had gotten written. It was a gift. A gift to me. Now a gift from me to anyone who takes the trouble to read it.

I trembled. I wept. For joy.

Saying Thanks Primes the Pump of Gratitude

There have been times when, if someone told me that life is a gift, I would have wanted to give it back. There was so much about life that I hated, so much pain, that I could not locate grace enough to stir the ashes of gratitude. But I said thanks anyway, and saying it helped keep the window open.

You never know when saying something that you

do not feel will prime the pump and get the feeling flowing. The line between pretending to feel something and beginning to feel it is, as C. S. Lewis put it, too thin for a moral bloodhound to sniff. Thanksgiving is the primal whisper of the human heart. And the whisper may be the prime that starts the flow.

Giving a gift to a giver is another fine way to say thanks. Not as a trade-off, but as an opening move in the minuet. Moving in what Donald Postema calls the "spiral of joy." It works well when we give the right gift, at the right time, in the right way. Here are some hints I learned from someone else somewhere along the way.

Don't be too quick about giving gifts. If we give a gift too soon after we get a gift from someone, we are probably giving it because we feel beholden. We don't like someone to have the advantage over us; we want to get even quickly. Better to bridle the urge and wait a spell.

Don't give the same type of gift you were given. He gave you a ticket to a Dodger game; give him a book. She took you to lunch; send her a lovely card. He helps you lay tile for your patio; invite him to dinner. If you give the same sort of thing you received, you are making your gift look like a payment in kind.

Don't give a gift that costs as much as the gift you received. If I give you a gift that costs as much as the gift you gave me, my gift smacks of a payment to balance accounts. A gift of lesser value than the one you received makes it clear that you are saying thanks, not getting even.

Sometimes the gift we get is so huge that there is nothing we could give that would express the thanks we feel. If your brother-in-law gives you a kidney that you need to survive, you are better off to give him your blessing and nothing else. If you try to repay him, you will forever be in his debt, and the burden will drain away your joy.

Now let's get back to getting ready for gratitude.

We Are Always Grateful for One Thing in Spite of Something Else

Every silver lining must have a cloud.

Is it decent for us to rejoice and be glad while life this day is hell for other people?

I drove up to Larry Den Besten's condominium in Santa Monica, a stone's throw from the Pacific shore, on a crystal-clear morning whose azure infinity above blessed my world below. And for a few seconds before going in, I was suffused with gratitude at being alive in the beauty of that day.

But I took the elevator to the seventh floor, where Larry was lying on a hospital bed in his condo, dying of cancer. I sat at his side, took his long fingers in my hands, cold skin draped on the twig-like bones that had once been his swift surgeon's servants. I looked into his sunken eyes and told him that I was grateful for his friendship. But the feeling of gratitude for my own life that had overcome me a few minutes earlier felt now like an indecency.

I walked a while on the narrow span of parkway between Ocean Avenue and the cliffs, a green stretch where the jogging young and sauntering old can watch a playful ocean tease the rippled Santa Monica sands. Here, too, the homeless people shuffle behind their borrowed shopping carts piled high with plastic bags filled with the private paraphernalia of the hopeless.

I looked into the eyes of the first man I met. Like Larry's, they were sunken inside the two holes drilled into the skull, mountings meant for gems; but his gems were without luster, his lenses were unfocused, as if there were nothing around them they wanted to see. Yet they guided his aimless body, unattached to person or place, to a sun-warmed spot for laying himself down to sleep. Again my gratitude for the gift of my own life turned sour on me.

How could I be grateful for my life when my friend's more illustrious existence was being devoured before it had a chance to age? How dare I be grateful for my full life while homeless men and women live hopeless on the streets? My gratitude became my shame.

The world is too bent for unshadowed joy.

And yet, if we wait for every beggar to have his horse, we shall never be grateful for a ride. If we wait for every person to be fed, we shall never be grateful for our daily bread. If we wait for every person in the world to have a roof, we shall never be grateful for the roof that covers us while we sleep. If we wait till no one ever dies, we shall never feel grateful for life.

It isn't just the retching on the other side of the tracks that mutes our songs of thanks. It's the sad stuff on our own side that puts up the "in spite of's" like barbed wire blocking the path of gratitude. In a world where somebody may, at any moment, rain on your parade; where if something can go wrong, it is likely to; where you may, at any corner, be driven up the wall; in this kind of world, gratitude comes to us in spite of travails and tribulations.

If we remember this we can be ready for gratitude even when the music stops.

Gratitude Comes to Us in the Wake of Anxiety

Your toddler wandered away from home. He's been gone for twelve hours, but the police just found him and he is fine. Your daughter was not hurt as badly in an auto accident as the doctors first thought. The lump on your breast is not malignant after all. Gratitude seizes you and fills you with its joy.

But we have to feel the anxiety before we feel the joy. Some of us are dedicated to escape from anxiety. We light up a cigarette. We blab. We watch anything flickering on the television screen. We whack a white ball around the turf. We eat cookies or drink a martini. Anything to escape anxiety. But we cannot feel the full joy of release from anxiety if we forever refuse to experience the pain of anxiety first.

Let me go back again to my experience in St. Cloud. What had gotten me ready for my seizure of joy? Two things.

First, I had been terribly anxious, even though I hadn't recognized it. Sometimes the worst anxieties fester below the surface. But they are there even if we don't recognize them.

Second, I had no escape hatches from anxiety. No television. No stereo. No human being to talk to or body to touch. No books to read. No wine to drink. The simplest escapes were out of my reach.

My anxiety readied me for gratitude. I would not have felt the force of joy had I used my normal escapes from being anxious. I was ready for gratitude; and when it came it possessed me, raptured me, released me.

Most people have undercurrents of anxiety in their lives. About whether life has a point, about guilt and death and a hunch that our lives are out of control. Anxieties about our children or the sharp pain in the chest we felt after jogging last week. And we hate anxiety so much that we do anything to escape it.

Our culture offers a syndicate of escapes from the anxieties it causes. But there is a catch: We cannot overcome anxiety by escaping it.

Could it be that we are better off to take our anxieties into our consciousness? To be alone with them in solitude? To surrender ourselves and the things we are anxious about to God? And then, if relief comes, to give it time to sink in and stir about in our minds until gratitude takes over.

It may take time for gratitude to overcome us. And

it may come only through suffering. We cannot control it. But we can give it space.

≫≪

The strongest and brightest of us is as fragile as a floating bubble, unsteady as a newborn kitten on a waxed kitchen floor. If we keep our footing in the shaky space between our arrival and departure from this world, we owe our survival—not to mention our success—to many other people who held us up and helped us crawl or fly or just muck our way through. And to God, who keeps breathing life into our lungs the way a child keeps puffing air into a leaking balloon.

We cannot force gratitude to dance inside us. But we can keep the windows open. We can be ready for gratitude when it comes.

For instance, we can celebrate our gifts in all their imperfections. We can prime the pump of gratitude by saying a thanks we do not feel when we say it. And we can permit ourselves to feel the deepest anxieties of life so that we can also feel the joy of release from them. Most of all, we can shape our feelings of gratitude by thinking straight about the primordial fact of existence: The only reason why any of us should exist at all lies in the mystery of why the Creator should have desired to share the gift of life.

We take our every step in the energy of mercy. We breathe every breath in the atmosphere of grace. We think every thought and feel every feeling through the power of creative love. We see each flower, taste each drop of water, sense the presence of each person around us, through the gift of consciousness. When we see all this with our inner eye, we will need no one to tell us we ought to be grateful.

CHAPTER 2

A Bit of Grit

The white people of New Orleans were scared. So were the black people. A federal judge had ordered the city to open its public schools to black children, and the white parents decided that if they had to let black children in, they would keep their white children out. They let it be known that any black children who came to school would be in for trouble. So the black children stayed home too.

Except Ruby Bridges. Her parents sent her to school all by herself, six years old: the first and, for a little while, the only black child to learn a lesson in a white New Orleans school.

Every morning she walked alone through a heckling crowd to an empty school. White people lined up on both sides of the way and shook their fists at her; they threatened to do terrible things to her if she kept coming to their school. But every morning at ten minutes to eight, Ruby walked, head up, eyes ahead, straight through the mob; two U.S. marshals walked ahead of her and two walked behind her. Then she spent the day alone with her teachers inside that big silent school building.

Robert Coles was curious about what went into the making of courageous children like Ruby Bridges, and went down there from Harvard to find out. He talked to Ruby's mother and, in his book *The Moral Life of Children*, he told us what she said. She observed, "There's a lot of people who talk about doing good, and a lot of people who argue about what's good and what's not good," but there were also some other folks who "just put their lives on the line for what's right."

A POWER OF THE HEART

What secret spring do people like Ruby Bridges drink from when the moment comes for them to act in the face of danger and trouble? Where do we get the inclination to turn our backs on safety and comfort and do the very thing we are afraid to do?

Courage is generated in that recess of the spirit we poetically call the heart (*courage* being a sister to *coeur,* French for "heart.") Courage is a power that surges from the heart into our wills, leads us beyond thinking and talking, and pushes us to do the right thing when we are terribly afraid that doing it could cost us more than we want to pay.

But how does the power get inside the human heart?

Some would say that it is an instinct we share with animals.

I have watched a long shot filly with undistinguished bloodlines languish behind a whole field of horses for a full turn, caught in seventh or eighth place, where the smart money expected her to finish. Then, having given nobody a hint of what she had in her, she makes a run for it. She surges, her slender legs pounding into the turf, pushing the massive barrel of her body through the thick of the pack. Her neck and her head pull her glistening chestnut bulk forward with heroic, rhythmic lunges. She reaches the leaders and then, with a final fury, finishes a fine nostril ahead of the pack.

From the underground of her animal psyche percolated a power that horse people call heart. It may be the same power that holds the beaten fighter on his feet and keeps him slugging, pounding, swaying, ducking; perhaps the fighter is drawing courage from the same animal instinct that a mother gopher draws on when she fights to save her young from a marauding coyote.

But there is more to it than the primal energy of the animal spirit.

Courageous People Will to Do What They Know They Have to Do

Ruby *could have* stayed home. She didn't *have* to go to school. And every one of the cowards who heckled and threatened her *could have* walked away from the crowd and come to Ruby's side. They *could have* if they had willed to do it. We do not *have* to be cowards. Shakespeare's Cassius was right:

> *Men at some time are master of their fates:*
> *The fault, dear Brutus, is not in our stars,*
> *But in ourselves.*

The power of the heart resides in the will.

Human Courage Comes from a Force Beyond Animal Instinct and Human Will

A white schoolteacher described what she saw when Ruby Bridges walked into school:

> A woman spat at Ruby but missed; Ruby smiled
> at her. A man shook his fist at her; Ruby smiled
> at him. Then she walked up the stairs, and she
> stopped and turned and smiled one more time!
> You know what she told one of the marshals?
> She told him she prays for those people, the ones
> in the mob, every night before she goes to sleep.

Robert Coles says that he had no luck with explaining the courage of black children like Ruby in accepted psychiatric terms.

> If I had to offer an explanation, though, I think
> it would start with the religious tradition of
> black people, which is of far greater significance
> than many white observers have tended to allow.
>   In home after home I have seen Christ's
> teachings, Christ's life, connected to the lives of
> black children by their parents. Such a religious

tradition connects with the child's sense of what
is important, as anyone knows who has been in
a black church and seen the look of pain give
way to the look of hope in countless faces.

Socrates taught that a person gets courage by being
taught it. But, when pressed hard, he conceded that
courage is "neither natural nor taught," but comes to
us "by a divine dispensation."

Yea, though I walk through the valley of the
shadow of death, I will fear no evil: for thou art
with me; thy rod and thy staff they comfort me.
(Psalm 23:4, KJV)

In any moment of need we may call on all three
springs: animal instinct, moral will, and faith in God.
We may pray for courage and find the answer in our
animal energy and our human wills.

THE MANY FACES OF COURAGE

Ruby Bridges's courage came from her heart, but it
traveled on her feet. Courage comes alive in actions.
How silly I would sound if I were to pound my chest
and roar that I have the heart of a lion, and yet run like
a frightened fawn whenever I smell a threat. The power
of the heart has got to have something to show.

But what sort of thing? The answer is simple:
almost any sort at all. You can show courage by advanc-
ing; you can show courage by retreating. You can show

courage by dying for a good cause; you can show courage by living for a good cause. You can show courage by saying no to compromise; you can show courage by making a heroic compromise. You can show courage by throwing off your yoke; you can show courage by bearing it. Courage comes to life in almost any shape or form.

There are, however, two basic forms of courage. One is acting well at the risk of deadly danger. The other is acting well when troubles are already upon us.

Take the first form. We look danger full in the face and do what we have to do in spite of it. We make a move, and by making it, we risk loss to ourself. Maybe death. Maybe something else very important to our life.

This is Ruby Bridges risking a lot of trouble to herself by walking to a white school. It's David meeting Goliath. An astronaut taking his first trip to the moon. A child taking her second trip to the dentist. A government secretary who lets it be known up above that there is corruption down below. When we expose ourselves to danger for a good cause, we show grit, valor, fortitude, or courage by any other name. This is what philosophers have called *aggressive courage*.

When we act with aggressive courage, we risk dying with a passion for living. G. K. Chesterton saw it as a baffling paradox. Courage, he said, is "a strong desire to live taking the form of a readiness to die. [The courageous person] must seek his life with a furious indifference to it; he must desire life like water and drink death like wine." Only if we desire to live is death a danger…and risking it a form of courage.

Take the second form of courage.

People show courage just by struggling long against present adversity. They do not risk death, they risk living. It takes a lot of courage just to hang on to life when the sullen days of a wearying winter are too long and dark to endure. We dig in daily, bear what we desperately do not want to bear, make no bones about not wanting it either, rage sometimes against the unfairness of it all—and yet we live with it, and now and then we even feel good about the tough life we live.

When sorrows whisper that living is a bigger burden than we can bear, it takes courage to look trouble full in the face and affirm our lives in spite of it. What we have here is *perseverance*, or what the apostle Paul was inclined to call *patience*. Plato called it *endurance*. Thomas Aquinas talked about a *passive* courage that is just as real as *aggressive* courage.

We often need this kind of courage as we get older, when our spicy juices turn to a sluggish syrup; when we feel in every joint a rusty resistance to healthy intentions; when our sexual drive is more memory than temptation; and we notice too often that too many of our old friends have died. It takes courage to celebrate life while numbering our days.

Some people need courage to get going in the first place. Philosopher Hannah Arendt once observed that courage "is in fact already present in a willingness to insert one's self into the world and begin a story of one's own." She was right. Hacking out a place for ourselves in the tough circumstances we were plunked into without having been consulted as to our preference—this, too, is courage.

Some people need unusual courage to commit themselves to a marriage long enough to turn a difficult relationship into a permanent partnership, in which two people can grow as separate individuals and deepen their oneness at the same time. But a woman with no marketable skills may need a lot of courage to *leave* a marriage that has become more brutal and demeaning than any human being should put up with.

Sometimes Only Courageous People Really Know Why It Took Courage for Them to Do What They Did

Tony Melendez once played the guitar for Pope John Paul II. Tony Melendez has no hands. He plays the guitar with his toes. The Holy Father thought it took a lot of courage for Tony to play the guitar with his toes. When Tony finished his piece, the pope bent down, patted him on the head quite papally, and said to him: "Tony, you are truly a courageous young man. Keep giving hope to people. Keep ministering."

Paul Longmore says that the pope was wrong about why Tony Melendez needed courage. It was not playing a guitar with his toes that took courage. What

Tony needed courage for was to live with purpose after the pope's church told him that it does not ordain disabled people to be ministering priests of the church.

Paul Longmore has hands, but he cannot use them. Nor can he sit up much; his back is severely curved. Yet he wrote a large, scholarly, and much-lauded book called *The Invention of George Washington*. He wrote it with his mouth, a pencil clenched in his teeth, pecking out letter after letter on a computer keyboard.

He does not think it took much courage to write a book with his mouth. It was just another one of the problems disabled people have to solve: how to eat a sandwich, how to take a bath, how to have sex, and how to drive a car. So, through trial and error, he solved the problem of how to write a book without using his hands.

What takes courage, Longmore tells me, is living with some hope in a society that seems bent on discouraging people who have disabilities. Take, for instance, the obstacles professional guidance counselors put in Paul's way:

> "Why do you want to get a Ph.D.? Nobody out there is going to hire you to teach."

> "I want to be a scholar."

> "Better forget it, son, it's too tough; they aren't going to hire you; find another way."

> "But I want to be a historian."

"I know, but you've also got to be practical. The academic world is too competitive for the disabled; find another way."

It is the awful heaviness of discouraging words that creates the negative need for courage.

Discouraging words almost beat my mother to the ground. She was a widow at the age of thirty, with five little ones to look after. An immigrant alone in the American world, she had no job skills, no work experience, and no pension to speak of. She needed the power of the heart to keep her brood alive and well while she was out most days polishing other people's floors. But the worst of it was the discouraging word she heard from our pious second- and third-generation American neighbors. Two women in particular took a keen interest in mother's struggle. One day they came across the street to tell her that she was not competent to take care of her children and that she should give up the two youngest for adoption. Only she knew how much courage it took to keep on believing that her neighbors were dead wrong.

Which takes us back to Tony Melendez. Playing a guitar with your toes does not take all that much courage. Any more than writing a book without hands. Or scrubbing people's floors when you want with all your heart to be there when your kids come home. Living with callous advisors, blind bureaucrats, a church that turns its back on disabled people who want to be priests, and putting up with discouraging words from ignorant neighbors—that is what takes courage for struggling people. This is what my friend Paul Longmore told me.

No Matter What We Do, to Count As Courageous We Need the Right Motive for Doing It

Aristotle said, "It is for a right and noble motive that the courageous [person] faces dangers and performs the actions appropriate to courage."

We can run into a burning house to save a child, which is courageous. Or we can run into a burning house to save our record collection, which may be craziness. Those odd folk who drop themselves over Niagara Falls in a barrel are daredevils, sure enough, but few of us call them courageous. A woman may risk her life because she hates life and wants, consciously or unconsciously, to end it. And a man could run straight into a buzz saw because he doesn't know what he is doing. Risking everything does not count as courage unless there is a good reason behind it.

Captain Ahab is a daredevil that Herman Melville created to show that grand acts can be poisoned by ignoble motives.

Ahab, a whaling man, hated Moby Dick, the great white whale. He hated with a fury like the ocean's own tempestuous rage. Why shouldn't he hate him? The whale had taken his leg. And Ahab was driven by gales of vengeance to get even for the loss. He put his life on the line to stain the ocean red with the blood of the white whale.

At the terrible end, in ultimate confrontation with his life's enemy, Ahab had an illumination into his soul's true motive, and he moaned to heaven: "Oh now I feel my topmost greatness lies in my topmost grief." Then, poised to hurl his harpoon in a last useless lunge against his hate, he cried: "From hell's heart I stab at thee; for hate's spite I spit my last breath at thee." The whale, wishing only to plow unhindered through his ordained home, turned his face against Ahab and destroyed him, his ship, and all his crew, save the one who lived to tell the tale.

We do not know, we cannot tell, what another person's deepest motives are. We cannot always be sure of our own. Our motives are seldom simple, seldom pure. Still, it is good to know that the word "courage" was invented for people who gamble with life while they love the life they risk, and take the risk for noble, though mixed, motives.

WALKING THROUGH THE SHADOWS

Tradition has always linked courage to a threat of dying. "Heroism," wrote Ernst Becker in *The Denial of Death,* "is first and foremost a reflex of the terror of death. We admire most the courage to face death; it moves us deeply in our hearts because we have doubts about how brave we ourselves would be."

Death comes in stages and degrees. There is the

final death that ends our walk on earth, releases our spirits, and sets our bodies in the ground. But we all die preliminary deaths on the way to the final curtain. These are losses, not of life itself, but of the precious fragments of life that give our lives meaning and make them worth living.

Let's talk first of that final death that puts someone in a grave.

One way to avoid a test of courage is to pretend we are not dying. And one way to pretend we are not dying is to deny that death is really death.

"Modern man," Becker says, "is drinking and drugging himself out of awareness, or he spends his time shopping, which is the same thing." Other people deny death by disguising it. They talk about death a lot, but they mask it and make the enemy look like a friend. Death becomes one of the seasons of life, late autumn perhaps, when the green leaves of summer turn color and begin to fall, a season with a brooding beauty of its own. But death is not one of the four seasons of life, it is the end of seasons.

We are discouraged from facing the inevitability of our dying because our culture lives by the myth of mastery and conquest. We prize ambition and power and success; we are taught to believe that the human mind can solve every problem, conquer every disease, and control every contingency. We are the Promethean society. People like us do not take well to inevitable defeat. But death is inevitable; it is appointed that every person should die. And it takes courage for a modern mind, fed on the myth that everything can be conquered, to face up to the reality that we shall all die.

I wish, however, to narrow the question to our own private fears of our own private dying. Why are we afraid? Why does it take courage even to think about our death? Three reasons come to mind.

We fear death because we lose so much by dying. We lose the people we love, our wives and husbands, our children, our friends. We lose our work, our games, our art, all the things we do that give us gladness. We cannot take them with us into the dark, dark night.

We fear death because somewhere beyond the dark night of dying there is a divine light that may expose us for what we really are; and we fear that Someone may see that we are not as good as we pretend to be.

We fear death because it is a dark door into a darker unknown. Or a vast bottom under a vast abyss. We may have a strong faith that it is good to go and be with the Lord in that unexplored place. But even faith does not remove the fearsome darkness of the passage.

These, it seems to me, are some reasons why death frightens us so much and why we need courage to face it.

We show courage, however, not only when we dare to die, but when we dare to live after we have died a preliminary death.

Living with our preliminary deaths is fearsome too, and it takes a good bit of courage to choose life while the very thing that makes us want to live is taken away. There are many ways of dying a preliminary death. Consider a few of them.

We Die Vocational Deaths

Michael Longejans was about to break through as a solo dancer in the San Francisco ballet when he discovered he had Parkinson's disease. He had to quit, and he died inside. Buck Bast, a twenty-game winner for the Pirates, lost his ability to get hitters out; he went back to pumping gas at a garage in North Carolina and died inside.

We Die Genetic Deaths

Here is a young couple trying to get themselves with child. Eric had been disowned by his family, and felt dead to his origins. So he desperately wanted a child to provide him with a future. But Greet, his wife, was not getting pregnant.

They learned to make love by the menstrual clock and, after a few years of scheduled copulation, Greet conceived.

But then she miscarried, had a hysterectomy, and by the cruel cuts of surgery was rendered forever barren.

When he learned the truth, Eric moaned: "I had no past and now I have no future. I have lost my life."

We Die When We Lose Someone We Love

"When she died, something died in me. Part of me is lying in her grave." It can happen, too, when someone is divorced. "Being his wife was my life, and now that he has left I am walking around dead inside."

We Die When Life Loses Its Meaning

A man wakes up one morning with a horrible hunch that the whole human scene, from the muddy beginning until now, is a cosmic accident doomed to end as a global garbage heap. His own life story now feels like a flutter in time, with no more significance to it than the buzzing of a horsefly around a pile of manure. He dies.

We go on breathing when we die our preliminary deaths, but part of us dies inside. And the other part has to decide whether it still wants to live.

Wherever we find people with the courage to affirm life in the midst of their preliminary deaths, we should celebrate. When we meet a woman who chooses to live a creative life even though she has to carry an oxygen tank around with her, we should pause to celebrate the mysterious power of the human heart we call courage. When we know a man with AIDS who manages against all odds to live with dignity among the people he loves as long as he can hold his body up straight, we should humbly thank God for his courage. When we know a woman who dares to go on living and loving with self-assurance after a surgeon slices away her breast, we should discreetly sing to her courage. If we had sense to notice the power some people discover within themselves to affirm the joy of living, we would turn each day into a festival.

ONLY FRIGHTENED PEOPLE HAVE IT

When I was a boy I had a notion that I might get to be a brave person one day if only I did not get so scared. To be afraid, I guessed, was to be a coward. Even the *Oxford English Dictionary* defines courage as "facing danger without fear." But the truth is more like this: Only people who are afraid have courage. Fear is to courage what breathing in is to breathing out.

Courage Is at Home in the Frightened Heart

The boy recruited to fight the Civil War—when a soldier still looked his enemy in the eye while he killed him—was instructed that a man of courage was never afraid to fight. So he believed that he was expected to run straight into the enemy's fire without fear of death. But in honest-to-goodness fact, he was scared to death. He was afraid of the bullets that were cracking his comrades' skulls like eggshells. He was afraid to go forward and he was afraid to go backward; but the fear of going backward was the stronger of his fears, so he ordered his feet to keep on marching toward an enemy waiting just over the hill with firm intention to shoot him dead.

He had courage all right, precisely because he was afraid. Yet, all the while, the poor soldier was ashamed of his fear because he thought that to be afraid was to be a coward, no matter how gallantly he soldiered. So, back in the Civil War, nobody—private or general—admitted he was scared.

The soldiers of the Second World War knew that

being afraid and having courage went together like being thirsty and taking a drink. John Steinbeck wrote that it was "the style" for a conscript to tell his buddies how scared he was. Ernie Pyle, the foot soldier's reporter, scotched the silliness that said courage and fear could not mix: "war scares the h—out of me. I guess it's because I don't want to die. But I know I'm not a coward." Maybe Sid Dumph put the lid forever on the romance of fearless courage when he wrote from Vietnam: "We were all scared every second, and we could never have made it if we didn't admit it to each other."

If you were not afraid to die, it would take no courage to doff your cap and ride upright into the enemy's fire. The courageous person, Thomas Aquinas wrote, is very much afraid, but "sets himself against this fear and turns upon the danger." Courage, I have heard tell, is fear having said its prayers. The question is, where do we get the courage to do the things we are afraid to do?

Hope Gives Us Courage to Do What We Are Afraid to Do

We fear and we hope at the same time. Fear lurks behind hope the way the dark side of the moon lurks behind its shining face. And hope answers fear the way the sun answers the darkness of the night.

An ordinary visit to a doctor is a little parable of fear and hope. We are afraid we might be sick, and we are afraid the doctor may tell us that we are very sick.

But we have a hope that if we are sick, the doctor can cure us. Fear says, "Don't go, you may get bad news." Hope says, "Go ahead, he may find a way to heal you."

If it is hope that encourages, the loss of hope is the death of courage.

Eugene O'Neill wrote a play, *The Iceman Cometh*, about a sad assortment of sadder drunks living together in a dingy hotel in the shabbiest part of town. What gave each of them courage to get up in the morning was a crippled hope that one day soon he would put the cork back in the bottle, check out, and take hold of life again.

A traveling salesman named Hickey came to the hotel now and then, and the men looked forward to his coming because he was usually good for a few laughs. But this time Hickey did not come for laughs. He came with a plan of salvation. They could be saved, he told them, only if they chucked their pipe dreams and surrendered to the truth: They were hopeless drunks.

They all believed him. Hope died. And one at a time they lost the courage they had for living.

Hickey is like those German philosophers who used to roll their eyeballs and sputter that humankind's only hope is to give up hope. For them life was hopeless, because life was a meaningless spin in the whirl of existence. The only courage we needed, they said, was the courage to live without hope.

The fact is that we get courage for living when we have hope that life will win.

Every historian I know agrees that people change their world only when they have hope that things can be better than they are. People do not revolt against tyranny because they are oppressed; oppressed people revolt when they have hope that freedom is theirs for the taking. Hungry people do not revolt because they do not have enough to eat; hungry people revolt when they have hope that their children can be fed.

A hope that half a century's repression could not strangle broke the yoke of bondage in Eastern Europe in the late twentieth century. Through the ages, Christian martyrs put their bodies on the block because they had hope that their souls would be better off for it. Mother Teresa kept giving life to poor souls on Calcutta streets because she kept spotting human hope breaking through them. Ruby Bridges walked alone through walls of spite because she had hope that right would win the fight. Simple people marched for civil rights in step with a simple song of hope—"Deep in our hearts, we do believe, we shall overcome some day"—and singing it put courage in their hearts.

Hope gives us reason to do the very thing we are afraid to do, because hope is faith in the ultimate triumph of what we struggle for. But hope does something even more wonderful. Hope not only gives us courage to struggle; it can give us power to overcome.

We are defeated sometimes. We get cancer, and the prognosis is that we will die. Now, it will take courage simply to face the chemotherapy or the radiation. And it will take courage to walk through the valley of the shadow of death. But, with hope, some people defy the prognosis and are healed.

In the human brain billions of neurons carry electrochemical signals to the countless receiving stations in the miracle called the human body. The message the neurons send out depends on the impulses they take in. My finger sends the neurons a pain message and the neurons flash an order to the finger: "Drop the hot pan!"

My spirit also sends messages to the neurons in my brain. For instance, my spirit sends a message that something funny is going on, and my neurons send back an order to laugh at it. My spirit sends a message that something sad is happening, and my neurons reply, "Why don't you weep?" And so when my spirit sends a message of hope to my neurons, my neurons cable back to my body: "Heal yourself."

Hope not only gives us courage to fight a disease, it gives us a better chance to win. Norman Cousins, after ten years at the medical center of the University of California in Los Angeles, wrote in his book *Head First* that it is not unscientific to speak of a "biology of hope." I believe Cousins is on to something.

But hope is not magic. It does not always defeat disease. At least one bad prognosis eventually comes true. We all die, no matter how much we hope to live.

Dietrich Bonhoeffer was a German pastor during the time of Hitler's dictatorship. From the beginning, Bonhoeffer saw the Nazis for what they were and risked everything to fight them. They finally arrested him and put him in prison. It was from there that he wrote *Letters and Papers from Prison,* which still inspire courage in those who read them. In one of the letters he penned this prayer: "Give me the hope that will deliver me from fear and faintheartedness." He was given hope. And hope gave him courage. But they killed him. And God did not come to save him.

The Question of Hope Almost Always Ends with the Question of God

Sometimes I am almost sure that God has gone on leave of absence. Or I fear that he is not on our side anymore. Hope answers that He *is* still here and that He *is* still on our side. God is on the side of life, not death. God is on the side of love, not hate. On the side of peace, against war. On the side of joy, against misery. This is hope's last stand.

This is what the resurrection of Jesus is about for me: hope for the ultimate victory of God. I am often afraid He may be losing the fight, but hope restores my faith that He will win. My head lobs darts of doubt at my heart. But then I join the chorus when hopeful people sing:

Peace is going to win, brother.
Oh yes, Lord.
Love is going to win, sister.
Oh yes, Lord.

Joy is going to win, children.
Oh yes, Lord.
Oh yes, Lord.

HOW COMMON PEOPLE EXPLAIN IT

Sooner or later each of us is offered a moment for courage. We will each stand at a crossroad sometime. And when we're there, we shall have to decide whether we will do the right thing, even if doing it means putting our lives on the line.

No one can decide for us. Others can teach us, others can inspire us, others can threaten us, but no one can act in our place. Each of us must finally do it alone.

When we do act, we will each have our own reasons. Courageous people have their own ways of accounting for their courage. They would all agree, if we pressed them, that they could do what they did because they had some hope that what they did would be worth the trouble. But they usually come up with other explanations, too—closer to the surface of their thoughts and just as real, if not as deep, as hope. Let's listen to some of them.

They Get Courage to Live Because They Love Life Too Much to Die

An Iowa farmer by the name of Rod, only thirty-one, had been married to a strong woman named Sylvia for just a few years. One day he and his dog were hunting pheasant near the South Dakota border. As he stalked through the dry cornfields, he tripped over his own dog. His gun went off and ripped away his genitals, and a chunk of his pelvis with them. Rod survived. But he could not believe that a man without the genitals he was born with was a real man.

Rod surrendered to his sorrow for a cold Iowa winter, and sank deep into a depression that felt hardly different from death.

But spring came back strong that year. When it came, Sylvia took Rod out each April morning to walk their undulating acres of black soil checkered with the green sprouts of newly risen soybeans. She took him to the barn to watch a heifer throw a newborn calf; she took him to the Baptist church to hear some gospel singing by a visiting choir of Pentecostals; and she even got him into a flat old rowboat with her to fish for some bass at Ingot Lake, some twenty miles away.

Sylvia gradually weaned Rod away from death by the sights and feelings of resurrection. And when his pastor asked him by what miracle he had been raised, he said, "Spring came and I just fell in love with life again."

Walking on this journey, we all get tired and discouraged, and sometimes very sad. There are abundant reasons for decent people to surrender to their sorrow. And when people dig into their strength and rise to unsung moments of courage, sometimes the only way they can explain it is that they love life too much to surrender to death.

They Get Courage by Remembering the Stories They've Heard

Eighty-two-year-old Sandor Ungvari is a gentle Hungarian scholar who stands so straight that you could drop a plumb line from his chin to his instep and the line would not touch his middle. Except for dreams that now and then bring back some terror from the past, he lives a fairly serene life in the Rocky Mountain cabin that, with his handsome wife, Els, he refashioned into a lovely mountain home. But it was not always serene for Sandor.

When the Nazi armies invaded Hungary in 1939, Sandor was marked for trouble by a book he had written called *Life and Death of Hungarian Nazism*. They arrested him, sentenced him, tortured him. But he survived the Nazis until the Communists came.

The Communists assumed that anyone the Nazis tortured would support the new regime. They were mistaken. Sandor organized an underground intellectual resistance, and in general became a nuisance the new regime could not tolerate. And so it was that in the first of many spy trials in postwar Hungary, he was charged with sixty counts of spying for the United States. They sentenced him to hang.

He did not hang. His lawyer cut a deal in which he signed over all of his property to the party and, in exchange, got his sentence changed to eight years in the Gherla prison. It was said that no one ever came out of Gherla alive. But Ungvari made contact with three Hungarian nationalist guards who helped him escape.

He got outside the walls, swam the ice-caked Szamos River that swirled around the prison island, and walked at night, his body matted with mud, from village to village. In each village he located a pastor who gave him the name and address of the pastor in the next town, and by means of this pastoral underground he finally made it to the Austrian border.

When I visited Sandor and Els on their mountain, I asked him: "Why did you do it? Why weren't you more politic, why did you have to resist so openly?"

What he said went like this: "It was my family. They were all resisters, right from the beginning—from Janos Ungvari, a Magyar galley slave, to Andreas Ungvari, who was a leader in the Hungarian Reformation. I heard their stories over and over all my childhood days. With such family memories, could I do anything else?"

When Plato's students asked how to teach courage to their children, he said that we should tell them stories. When Hebrew fathers told their children the stories of how God led their ancestors out of bondage, courage seeped into the hearts of the sons and daughters. And the stories ordinary parents tell their children about the odd heroes in their ordinary families stir the alchemy of courage in their ordinary children.

Some Courageous People Say They Had No Choice

They do not decide to be courageous. A moment simply comes to certain kinds of people, and there is no escaping what they have to do.

Els Ungvari, Sandor's wife, was twenty-three in 1940 when she was in Rotterdam training as a social worker. She was attached to an orphanage where, among others, Jewish children lived. She had gotten used to waking up to the drone of bombers in the sky; but one morning, in May of 1940, they were closer.

It's for us this time, she thought.

That morning the airport was bombed; next day the whole city; then came the truckloads of Nazi soldiers; and in a matter of days, the burned-out city of Rotterdam was under German control. Holland surrendered. Els hiked across the back country to her home and joined the Dutch underground.

Because of her earlier experience with Jewish children, Els was assigned to go to Amsterdam. There, Jewish families were herded up to wait for the freight trains that would take them to concentration camps in the east. Her job was to persuade terrified parents to turn over their precious children to her. She was to take the children, three at a time, on the train with her to the neighborhood of Nymegen, three hours away, where they would be hidden in a monastery. Some of the parents refused, and took their children with them to die. Others, who had a hunch what was in store for them, entrusted their little ones to her and went on to die without them.

On the train the children were forever on the edge of exposing Els. Abi dropped his pants and displayed his circumcision, a sure giveaway in a country where no male Gentile was circumcised. Alex blurted out to a man in the next seat: "I'm Jewish. Are you Jewish too?" Hannah was making a fuss and was told to settle down. "Why?" she pouted. "It isn't Shabbat today."

Els was eventually arrested, questioned, beaten, let go, arrested again, jailed, released. It was cat and mouse, and she was always under surveillance. She made it to the war's end, working in the underground until the liberation of Holland.

When I visited her and Sandor in their mountain home, I asked her, as I asked her husband: "Why did you do it? Why did you go on and on, month after month, risking your life for a few Jewish people you did not know? What kept you at it?"

"I had no choice."

"But didn't you have a choice? Not everyone did what you did."

"Maybe they had a choice. Not I. For me, there was no other way: Either you are for God and the good, or you are for evil. I had no choice. I did some terrible things, too, things that look evil to me now. But I had to do the terrible things, because I had no choice but to be against evil."

So it is with courageous people when they see other people—their fellow human beings—in deep trouble. They don't calculate the costs and weigh the odds and finally decide to be heroic. They simply follow the lead of their deepest impulses and do what they have to do.

Courageous People Find Courage in Community

I have heard it said that, of all sports, the supreme test of character is the marathon run. In the marathon every runner is on his or her own, alone with terrible aches, alone with doubts, and alone, sometimes, with secret longings to drop out, lie down, and let the pain go away.

But when I watched my son Charlie run cross-country races, I learned that behind the lonely race was a runners' community. Off-track the runners formed an inner circle of commitment to each other—a breed apart, unlike other athletes. They knew it, and their sense of it made them comrades. At the end of the race, the person who came in first would run back several hundred yards to plead with the stragglers to hang in and finish strong.

They hugged each other's sweating bodies, bent over, heads below their hips. And, in a kind of runners' Eucharist, they took comfort from each other in their shared gratitude for having gotten through another run.

While it's true that nobody else can have courage *for* us, behind individual acts of courage there is usually a community of people. Courage is contagious. It spreads when we get close to each other.

The American psychologist Rollo May is sure that the source of courage goes back to the community of the family. If a person is a coward, a habitual coward, he writes, it "seems to come from an early rejection, an early feeling that the mother will not support her child and may even turn against him in his fight. Such a person finds it inconceivable that others would support him and that he is also fighting for them." But those people who, from the start, trust that the others in their family will not let them down when the crisis comes— these people are likely to act bravely for others.

Of course it takes some courage merely to be a member of a real community. To be honest within a group, to have the power to reveal our weaknesses, to have the self-control to speak in criticism and yet not in anger with people whom we need and love, this is courage. Once we are members of a real community, we gain from that very community a new source of courage. For in a community, we can find hope. And hope is where courage begins.

A Memory of Cowardice May Be the Birth of Courage

We all lose our nerve sometimes and slink away from what we fear. And we can get discouraged all over again whenever we remember the time our heart failed us. And yet, later on, the memory of our cowardly moment can move our heart toward courage.

One spring day, when I was thirteen, I got a letter in the mail that told me I had been chosen to be a camper—courtesy of the local Kiwanians—at Camp

Pendalouon. Free! Pendalouon was a boys camp where middle-class boys from Muskegon, Michigan, went for a fortnight of character building during the lazy summer.

The kids who went to camp were uppercrust, the sons of merchants and doctors, not my kind, and I was afraid that I would be a lonely charity case among them. But still, against the current of my fear, on an August Monday morning I lugged my gear downtown and waited alone at the curb for the camp bus. I stood a few steps outside the closed circle of bragging, laughing Pendalouon veterans, a foreigner and a freeloader among them.

Once in the bus I hoped we would crash and all of us would get hurt and they would call off camping for that session. But no luck. We arrived on time, disgorged, and I was there, an alien from another world, at Camp Pendalouon. They pointed me to Cabin Old Crow, and I walked over, knowing with fear's certitude that I would be rejected and despised when I got there.

I pushed open the screen door, dropped my bag near an empty bed, and was given an instant welcome that dissolved almost all of my fear. The veterans of Old Crow were plotting their strategy for the session, and they took me into the huddle right off the bat. I was at camp, and from the start I was an insider.

Before we had a chance to put our bags under the bunks, however, we were bugled together for a camp-wide powwow. The camp director, Mr. Mosher—Moses to old hands—explained that they had overbooked and that everybody who signed up had shown up, which put them two bunks short. He needed two volunteers to go home and come back the next session.

Moses looked hard and straight at me. His eyes told me: "Charity cases are expected to volunteer." I glanced around. The boys from Old Crow were passing signals: *Nobody* volunteer. I didn't.

I hunched my back and slouched toward Old Crow.

I determined to make it up to Moses by being a capital camper. I made my bed army style. I stuck close to our leader on every hike and asked him a lot of sincere questions about the local fauna. I mucked my way through crafts, tried to braid some strips of leather into a belt, Indian style, and settled in the end for a watch fob. I never griped about the food, gave nobody any trouble.

The last night around the campfire, Moses handed out ribbons to the campers he and the counselors selected as outstanding examples of the Pendalouon spirit. They invented ribbons for about everything anybody could be good at: most inspirational camper, most cooperative camper, most improved camper, most cheerful camper, most punctual camper, most anything a kid could be credited with to show his parents that camping had done him some good.

Just about everybody at camp got a ribbon for something.

Except me. No ribbon for me. Not for anything.

When the morning came, I packed my duffel bag

in shame. On the way back to town a camp counselor told me why Moses had sent me home without honor: It was my ungrateful refusal to go back home when Moses asked for volunteers.

But I wasn't ungrateful; I was just afraid. I was afraid that next time around I would be a nobody, an outsider, a stranger among the wellborn. I could not hope to strike it rich in Old Crow twice in a row. My hopeless fear made a coward of me. I never forgot it.

Years later I read a letter that encouraged me some. It was from Screwtape, Satan's lieutenant in *The Screwtape Letters* by C. S. Lewis. On the devil's business, as usual, he wrote to his apprentice, Wormwood, that people who do cowardly things are often so ashamed of themselves that they get converted. So he suggested that Wormwood not try too hard to tempt people to be cowards: "It is possible to lose as much as we gain by making your man a coward; he may learn too much about himself." As if to prove Screwtape's point, Winston Churchill once told his brother, "Being in many ways a coward—particularly at school—there is no ambition I cherish so keenly as to gain a reputation of personal courage."

◀ ▶

If we lived in a world where the people who did the right thing always got the glittering prizes, nobody would need courage. Or, if we lived in a paradise where nothing ever threatened us, we would not need courage. But in the real world we need courage, because we fear the possibility of pain and loss and death.

To do right when doing it *risks* final death and to do well *while* we are dying our partial deaths—this is courage.

Much depends on our spiritual preparation. Some of us were encouraged by our parents, by the memories of our family or our community, or by the hope that comes from childhood faith. But courage comes to those who have prepared themselves for it. For instance, we all decide sometime whether we believe that doing right is more important than what we may lose by doing it.

Few of us decide ahead of time to be people of courage. We don't say, "Well, since I've given up jogging, I think I shall take up courage this year." At least not the way we might plan to take a European trip or resolve to go on a diet. It is only when the moment of crisis comes that we discover whether we actually have the power of the heart.

CHAPTER 3

Some Simple Integrity

In the bad days of Salem, Massachusetts, in 1692, good people were accused of consorting with the devil and spiriting death into their neighbors' souls. The only escape for the innocent was to confess to crimes they had not committed. So innocent women saved their lives by admitting guilt that was not theirs. And honest women who could not lie were hanged by the neck. People no longer knew who they were or what was expected of them.

Except for Rebecca Nurse. She knew who she was. She knew what she expected of herself.

Rebecca stood accused of killing newborn children with a witching spirit. In the courtroom wild-eyed girls screeched terrible things and pointed their fingers at her. And the rest of the people wept at the dreadful things they heard.

The god-fearing, devil-believing judge said to Rebecca: "It is awful to see your eye dry when so many are wet."

"You do not know my heart," she replied. "I never afflicted no child, never in my life. I am as clear as the child unborn."

The good John Proctor, an honest man, a man of

independent mind, was said to be Rebecca's partner. Proctor confessed to a guilt that never was his. He had a wife and a son to care for. When Proctor told his loving lie, the judge dangled his lie in front of Rebecca's conscience:

"Now, woman. Will you confess yourself with him?"

"Why, it is a lie, it is a lie; how may I damn myself? I cannot, I cannot."

She would not be herself if she lied, and she could not now become another woman, not at her age, not with her character. So there she said it, "I cannot, I cannot."

Proctor was not old; he had time to find his real self again.

But Rebecca was another kind of person. She had written an honest story with her life and, so close to finishing it, she could not now become a different kind of person. She had to write it her way until the end, and her way was the way of truth. But they took Rebecca outside and hanged her by her wrinkled neck.

OWNING OUR OWN STORIES

Rebecca Nurse came to life in Arthur Miller's biting play *The Crucible* to tell us what integrity is about. Integrity is a bigger thing than telling the truth. It is about *being* a certain kind of person. It is about being people who know who we are and what we are, and it is about staying true to what we are even when it could cost us more than we should have to pay.

Think of yourself as someone who is writing a story out of the bits and pieces of your life. You are both the author and the main character. And you are here on earth to try to write an honest story, a continuing story—not an unconnected collection of episodes, but a real story about a real person who somehow stays in one piece, inside and out, all the way to the end.

To write a real story, the first thing we have to do is own the story we are given to write. To own anything involves at least two things. First, we identify ourselves with what we own and say, "This is my story. If you want to know me, you must know my story; and if you know my story, you really know me. I *am* my story." Second, we take responsibility for what we own and say, "What comes of my story is up to me. This is my plot to take credit for, mine to take blame for, mine to own up to."

We own our stories when we are willing to accept the parts we cannot control and then do whatever we can with the rest. We own our stories when we can admit to their ugly sides, their stupid and crazy sides. We own our stories, too, when we celebrate their beautiful aspects, their smart sides and their good sides. We own our stories when we keep holding on to them, even when we feel as if the story we are writing is a bore or gets so confusing we don't know what to make of it.

Nobody writes a simple story. We weave it with threads of our maniacally selfish streaks, our ugly impulses, our lust and our hate; but we also sew it together with the thread of love and courage and a simple ambition to make something of ourselves. We take ownership of one chapter and then another, each in its own time, each in its own way, until we round off our story, whole, in one piece.

We own our stories a phase at a time. Let us walk through some of the phases together.

We Own the Raw Material We Were Given

We all write our stories out of the raw material somebody else has given us. We take what we get, and then try to write a good story out of it—the way a poker player plays the game with the cards someone else deals him.

To begin with, we were dealt our parents. We were stuck with whomever we got, and there was nothing for us to do but to get going on our stories with whatever raw material they gave us.

I remember the Friday afternoon Doris and I walked into Bethany Home and, for the first time, met Cathy, a chunky girl child of seven months, who, though she was never given a say in the matter, would soon be our adoptive daughter. She was bawling like an amplified saxophone, her eyes shut against a world of strangers, her face puffed like a miniature Alfred Hitchcock. We picked her up, plunked her down into our game, and dealt her a hand she never had a chance to refuse.

We decided who her brothers and friends would be, where she would live, what sort of school she would go to, what God she would be taught to worship, and who would surround her every waking moment with their loving, nagging, angry, confusing, caring, careless, stupid, and wise parental devotion. She had no options.

And before we came along, somebody else had provided her with a genetic legacy. Two people came together in a moment of passion and then and there bankrolled or handicapped her with a genetic blueprint of her future. The same thing happens to us all. Some of us inherit a genetic fortune. Others begin with a budget deficit. Either way, we take what we get.

We can write honest stories only if we come to terms with whatever raw material we were given.

For some it all comes as a gift. For others childhood is a nightmare too horrible to remember. For almost all of us it is a mixed inheritance. But whether we remember them in thanks, look back on them in rage, or recall them in a crosswind of conflicting emotions, our parents are the only parents God will ever give us and the raw material we get from them is the only grist we will ever have for grinding out our stories.

If we have enough imagination, we may understand that our parents were limited by the raw materials they got from *their* parents. So we accept them as they were with an indulgent grace. And what we cannot understand or accept we may need to forgive. Indeed, for some, the toughest part of owning our

stories is forgiving our parents for giving us such pain
to begin our stories with. But if we are going to take
ownership of our stories, we must forgive them in spite
of everything—and then go on to write a good story
out of whatever material they gave us to work with.

We Own Our Wounds

I have never made total peace with the suffering in my
story; there is a dreamer in me who wants a world
where nobody gets badly hurt. The adult in me knows
that it is our destiny to suffer. We are sensitive souls
matched up with bodies prone to pain. We are bound
sometime to get hurt. In at least one chapter of our
story, pain will grab us in its claws, pin us down, tear at
our flesh, and pierce our heart.

It is natural to want suffering to be over and done
with. We may resign ourselves to writing one chapter
of our life story in pain or in tears. But, having written
it, we want to leave it behind us forever and feel the
wound no more.

I will deal here with two kinds of pain: the loss of
someone we love, and the experience of betrayal and
disloyalty by someone we love. First, the pain of loss.

Some people are chronic mourners. These perpetual grievers fuel an eternal flame of sorrow so that
everyone will notice how deep their grief is. They keep
their dead loved ones' clothes pressed in the closet,
their beds made, their toys in place. They rage when
the close friends of their dead spouses do not remain

close friends. They cannot move on to write a new chapter by themselves.

But at the moment I am not worried about addictive mourners. I am concerned with the person who, once having been hurt by loss, expects the pain to go away completely, wants to move on unscathed and put away suffering, the way our grandparents put away their black arm bands when the proper mourning period was over.

Our culture tells us that to carry our suffering with us is a weakness. We are made to feel a little ashamed if we go on feeling pain after the prescribed amount of weeping is done. So, to escape our shame, we disown our pain. We make believe it is no longer part of us.

But we *are* wounded, forever wounded; and to disown our wound is to be untrue to ourselves. We cannot move on from a suffering chapter of our stories without carrying the wounds with us into the next chapter. The pain of one chapter becomes the scar of the next.

A long time ago Doris and I lost our only biological child. We suffered together. But each of us also suffered alone. I raged; she accepted. But when mourning time was over, I went on as if I had left my grief behind me.

Recently I visited the small spot of ground at the end of a graveyard where we buried his small body so many years ago. I was flooded again by my old sorrow. My grief surprised me, embarrassed me. I thought it had died and left me. Where did it come from, this old sorrow?

It came from within me; it came from the wound

that had been a part of me all these years, inflicted a long time ago. The terrible pain is long gone, but the wound remains. Wounds can be reopened. All it takes is a fresh reminder. And it is honest and therefore healthy to own the wound, to let it identify us, to tell us who we are; for it is part of us forever.

Then there is the other kind of suffering, the unfair and deep pain we feel when someone betrays us, lets us down, brutalizes or demeans us. A parent molests us. A spouse is unfaithful. A friend is disloyal. Most of us will feel unfair pain sometime, if we just live long enough. This pain too leaves wounds that become part of who we are.

Some people hang on to their pain out of a sense of fairness. The person who hurt them does not deserve to be forgiven. So they will not allow the healing of a pain they did not have coming in the first place. Strange fairness, this, to condemn ourselves to perpetual pain that we do not deserve. But my concern here is not with people who either cannot or will not forgive.

I am concerned with people who do forgive and who expect that forgiving the person who hurt them will automatically remove the wounds.

People who forgive often have unrealistic expectations about the relief they will feel. They expect that once they have forgiven the person who hurt them, they will never feel the pain again. But forgiving does not take away our wounds; once wounded by another's unfairness and betrayal, we are forever wounded persons.

When we forgive we free ourselves from bondage to bitter memories. We release ourselves from the acute, wrenching nausea of betrayal. We begin a process of healing. But we do not take away the wound. Not ever. Our pain has been grafted onto our very beings. We will carry a residue inside of us as long as we live. Any chance reminder can open the wound again. And the pain will come back for a little while.

It takes courage to own our wounds, but we gain something important if we do. I believe that I have been more aware of other people's wounds since I discovered that the wound of my own pain is still part of me. I believe that anyone who is able to own the wounds that remain after forgiving someone who bruised them is better equipped to overcome similar pains in the future. And better able, too, to help other hurting people overcome theirs.

Crucial to everything is the integrity we gain by owning our wounds as we own ourselves.

We Own Our Ogres

A great psychologist, Lee Travis, looked straight through me once and said, "Lew, you've got a murderer inside of you." He was right; I could kill. Well, maybe I couldn't actually wring somebody's neck, but I could wiggle my nose and render certain persons painlessly evaporated. I know that I have impulses to shove people out of my life as if they were inanimate objects, to consume them with my lust as if they were edibles,

and to turn on anyone who threatens my self-esteem.
My ogre, myself.

Mostly, though, my ogres settle for shallow mischief. Not deadly, but still very mean.

One ogre I particularly despise, and yet must own,
chokes off gladness and stifles my celebration when my
friends succeed too much. An honest man once said,
"Every time my friends succeed, I die a little." I know
what he means. I love to applaud strangers. And I want
my friends to do well too, mind you, particularly when
they are playing another game than mine. But, when
they are going after the same good things I want, I am
not elated as I should be when they get the prizes while
I am only mucking through.

My ogres are mean. But, if I am going to write an
honest story, I've got to factor them into the inventory
of my self.

Ogre ownership can trip us into unbearable shame
or guilt. I have so many ogres inside of me, I could
walk through the dictionary and come up with a handful of labels for my tangle of ogres. A few of them
would answer to names like mean, cheap, hypocritical,
self-righteous, lustful, prudish, vulgar, stingy. They are
my menagerie of ogres, my collection of masked selves.

How can I own my shabby selves, identify them as
parts of the real me, without being ashamed of myself?
Let me make a few suggestions.

First, my ogres are not my *whole* self. I have several
beautiful selves too, and they constitute the real me as

genuinely as my ogres do. I am a mix. A pretty good person is *always* a mix.

Second, they are my *potential* self. That is, they are what I have in me to become. Hints of what I could actually be. They are me, but they are me the way a seed is a weed.

Third, they are usually the *unexpressed* me. I do not put all my impulses into action. And there is a big gap between an impulse and an act. I know people who believe that it is as evil to nurse a rage against someone as it is to slug him with a lead pipe. I disagree. The person I only wish were dead can still go home at night and play basketball with his children. So when I feel a wish that someone were dead, I am not on a moral par with a murderer. True, my ogres are not innocent. But my fantasies do not kill. As long as they stay where they are.

Fourth, I am *totally* forgiven and affirmed by God. The shadow side of me is the forgiven side. The light side is the affirmed side. So, as a whole person, ogres and all, I am loved. And why, then, should I not own myself, ogres and all?

We Own the Bad Chapters

There are some bad chapters in everybody's story. We have all sewn ugly stitches into the fabric of our selves. Sometimes we would like to press a button and erase them the way we purge the memory of our computers. But life is not equipped with a delete key. And there's the rub.

Some of us take too much responsibility for the bad chapters and shackle ourselves to guilt for everything about them. We excuse ourselves for nothing, take the blame for everything. Owning too much becomes our damnation.

The classic example of how an inflated sense of responsibility for our past can damn us is the tragedy of King Oedipus, the son of Laius, King of Thebes. Oedipus was taken away from his royal home soon after he was born, and grew up in a far country. When he was a young man, he happened, on a journey, to encounter a stranger at a crossroad. A misunderstanding arose between them and they drew their swords; Oedipus fought the stranger, and, being younger and stronger, he thrust the stranger through. What he didn't know was that the stranger was his father, the king.

Afterward, Oedipus came to Thebes. There had been a crisis in the city and, by his wisdom and strength, he saved the city from its troubles. Acclaimed by the grateful people as the worthy successor to Laius, he was crowned king of Thebes and, not knowing who she was, took the king's widow—his own mother—to be his wife.

Oedipus ruled Thebes well, but eventually a plague befell the city. A certain seer knew who Oedipus was and believed the plague was a judgment on the city for his sins. He revealed to Oedipus the tragic wrongs he had done.

On hearing the truth, the proud and honest king decreed his own dark doom:

Darkness!
Horror of darkness enfolding
memory of evil deeds I have done!
Why should I see?

He then went into his chambers and tore out his eyes with his own fingers and wandered the rest of his dark days in the endless abyss of his merciless accountability. Oedipus owned his past, took total responsibility for wrongs he did in innocence, refused to excuse himself for anything, and forgave himself nothing.

Consider now the story of Raskolnikov, told by the great Russian novelist Fyodor Dostoyevsky in *Crime and Punishment*. Raskolnikov murdered a wretch of a woman in cold blood for no good reason except to prove that, being a superman, he could live above the law of God. He knew exactly what he was doing. He did not act in innocent ignorance; he was no Oedipus doing terrible things that he could not be held responsible for. He was responsible, but he would not admit it. Oedipus accepted more blame than he should have; Raskolnikov grasped for a way to avoid any blame for what he did. He did it, he said, "through some decree of blind fate."

His resurrection came through Sonia, who loved Raskolnikov and brought him to the police to admit his crime, though in his mind he still refused to own his act; he still found excuses for himself. He blamed it on the dark whims of fate. In prison, however, he came gradually and with great agony to see the deep falsity in his excuses. One day he fell at Sonia's feet inside the prison wall and accepted her love. There, in love's patient power, he found the courage to own his own great crime. And, as he owned it, he also seized the only remedy that exists for a past chapter that we own and yet cannot change: forgiveness.

Oedipus and Raskolnikov are uncommon examples of what ordinary people do with their commonplace sins and mistakes. Oedipus took responsibility for tragedy that was not his doing, and thus owned too much and was crushed under its burden. Raskolnikov—who earlier disowned his act by blaming it on his tragic fate—finally owned his horrible crime and accepted forgiveness for it. Most of us are inclined to be either an Oedipus or a Raskolnikov. If we are overly conscientious, we take responsibility for more than we deserve. If we are afraid to be guilty, we weasel our way out of blame.

Too much responsibility destroys us. So does dishonest denial of our past. Only honesty answered by grace can free us.

We Own Our Commitments

Once we are well underway, we begin new chapters in our story by making significant commitments.

I speak a promise. "I will be there with you." Just a few words, mere words, words that I do not comprehend when I speak them; yet they flip from my lips straight into another person's memory to create a bond between us that neither of us will easily break. And so it is that my commitment nudges me into a new chapter of my story.

My commitments link what I am today with what I was in my past. When I remember them, I am remembering who I am.

Hannah Arendt reminds us in the closing chapters of her book *The Human Condition* that the stakes are high.

> Without being bound to the fulfillment of our promises, we would be condemned to wander helplessly and without direction in the darkness of each person's lonely heart, caught in its contradictions and equivocalities.

To wander helplessly in the darkness of our own lonely heart, *caught* in its contradictions, trapped in equivocality. This is to lose our integrity.

The American psychologist Erik Erikson taught us that to write a real story a person needs to have "the capacity to commit himself to concrete affiliations, to abide by such commitments, even though they call for significant sacrifice." One way to weave our chapters into a whole story that we can make some sense of is to make commitments and to own the commitments we make. If we don't have the courage to own our commitments, we gradually lose touch with who we are and what our story is about.

We Own the Story We Were Given to Write

Some people, as they get into the last chapter, lose faith that their story was worth writing. They think they should have written a more successful or heroic story than the one they were given to write. Two syndromes make it hard for us to own our story when we get close to the final chapters: the Walter Mitty syndrome and the Atlas syndrome.

The Walter Mitty syndrome gives us fantasies of stardom: Everybody knows our name, recognizes us at the airport, names public parks after us. But when we get old we know the fantasies have faded; we will never be a star, not even a little asteroid in a big sky. How can we own such a disappointing story?

Then there is the Atlas syndrome. Atlas was the Greek god who carried the whole world on his shoulders. With this syndrome we half suspect that we, not God, have the whole world in our hands—or on our backs. We hold ourselves responsible for most of the ills in the world, and we cannot own our story because we did not do enough to save the world from its sins and tragedies. Well, perhaps not the whole world, but we certainly should have saved our own children from their troubles. We cannot entrust the world to God, or our children to themselves. Everything is somehow our fault. How can we own our story when we let the world down?

The two syndromes strike both the great and the humble.

Among the great was John Quincy Adams. This

man spent his life in his country's service, once as president, before that as ambassador to Russia and Britain, and afterward as one of the better congressmen Washington has ever seen. But this is what he wrote in his diary near the end of his career: "My life has been spent in vain and idle aspirations, and in ceaseless rejected prayers that something beneficial to my own species should be the result of my existence."

Among the humble was my mother. She was a great human being, though you'd never know it to listen to her. How could a young woman of thirty—widowed in the twinkling of an eye, who could hardly speak the English language, and had no skills to offer the marketplace, or relatives to lend a hand, or food stamps to put some potatoes on her table—how could she have fed five rambunctious kids and brought them up to earn an honest living in the fear of the Lord if she hadn't been a woman of quality? If any person had a right to look back on her life and say, "It was tough going, but I did what I had to do," she did.

One afternoon, getting close to her dying time, we sat together in her hospital room and talked more freely about the old days than we used to do. She was caved in, bone tired, hands folded on the white bedspread, eyes moist, lips indecisive. And she said:

"I am so glad that God forgives all of my sins. Oh, Lewis, I have been a great sinner, you know."

"Come now, mother, you worked so hard you didn't have the time to do any real sinning."

"But it's true, Son, a great sinner. I've been a great sinner."

"Name me a sin. One little sin."

"I can't remember any sins just now. But what does that matter? I know I've been a great sinner."

She meant what she said about being forgiven. But what she really wanted me to hear was the great sinner part. She wanted me to know that she did not consider her story worth anybody's owning. If her life story were a book, she would not have wanted her name on the jacket.

Let me tell you about John Maakgeld. He is a plain man, but he can tell you what I mean by owning our story once we've gotten most of it written.

John Maakgeld lived most of his life in garbage. It began with his father. When Theodore Maakgeld came to this country, he settled in Cleveland as a helping hand on a garbage truck in the days when garbage was hoisted onto dump trucks over a human shoulder. His boss dropped dead at the dump one day, so Theodore bought the truck from his widow. Until the day he died he earned a decent living by carting garbage from uptown restaurants to the landfills on the edge of town. As soon as his shoulders were big enough, John Maakgeld helped his father heave the garbage from the cans to the truck and then off again.

It did not take John long to figure out that there was more money to be made if he could get his hands on more than one truck some day, hire drivers, and keep several of them going at the same time. Before he was thirty he managed to get four trucks on the road, and figured he was on his way to big things in garbage. But three bad things happened to him along the way to the top of the heap.

First came a meeting with a Cleveland chapter of the mob. They told John that nobody could haul garbage in Cleveland without paying for protection. But John said he figured on being an exception to the rule. A week later somebody stole one of his trucks, loaded it to the hilt with fresh manure, backed it into his garage, and blew it up with dynamite. This persuaded John that paying tribute was a necessary evil in garbage hauling.

The second bad thing that happened was the Vietnam War. His son Ted was drafted, but he had moral feelings about not going. He wanted to be a conscientious objector and run away to Canada. John believed that when a young man's country calls him to fight a war, that person has to go, whether it's the war of his choice or not. Anybody who ran away was no son of his. Ted was shamed into the draft and went to Vietnam. He had only been there a couple of months when a squadron of American fighter planes accidentally strafed his platoon. Ted died by military mistake.

The third bad thing happened to John's wife, Lanie. Lanie's left leg suddenly wouldn't do what she told it to do; and, two years after Ted got killed in the war, Lanie was told she had multiple sclerosis. She needed a lot of care, and it changed John's life.

Garbage began to stink. He felt like a coward for doing business with crooks. The war turned bad, and Ted's dying lost its point. So did hauling garbage. And now Lanie was sick and was going to get worse. He stayed in the business because he was fifty and didn't know how to do anything else. But he sold off four of his five trucks, kept only one, drove it himself, finished the run by noon, and dedicated his afternoons and evenings to Lanie.

John is in his seventies now. Lanie is gone. He mostly pokes around in his Sears cords and rag-wool sweater, cooking meals, cleaning the house, and keeping his Buick tip-top. If you got him to talking about the story he wrote, you would get a stream of thought that goes something like this:

"How do I feel about the life I've lived? I'm not complaining; not ashamed either. Getting rid of garbage is important. People don't think about that until it piles up. I wish to God I hadn't paid off those crooks. But I did it, so what can I do? I wish to God I had never talked Ted into going to war. It seemed right to me then, and given who I was and how I felt about this country, I'd probably do it again, but I'm sorry I did.

"What I believe is this: My life is one little stitch in the sleeve of God's big pattern. Lanie always said that I did pretty good with what He gave me to work with.

And she did a lot to get me to believe that God forgave me for my foul-ups. I'm grateful for that and I'm settling for what I've had and what I've done."

Garbage man! There is, it seems to me, some integrity to the way he owns his story.

Having a story to write is why we were born. Without a real story, we are hardly a person at all. We have to own our story, take responsibility for it, and claim it all as ours—the bad chapters and the good—in the sure knowledge that God will forgive us the bad ones and set us free to write better ones in the time we have left.

AN UNCORRUPTED CONSCIOUSNESS

Huck Finn saw an accident, and a fine white lady asked him whether anybody got hurt. Huck reassured her: "No'm, killed a nigger." Which relieved the gentle lady considerably. "Well, it's lucky because sometimes people do get hurt."

What's going on here? What's going on is that the lady would not let herself know what she really did know: that black people were people, just like her. Black people talked the way only people can talk, they wept as only people can weep when they sorrow, they loved each other with a love only people can feel. She knew this. But she corrupted her consciousness; she refused to know what she knew.

We all do it, one way or the other. We condense reality to suit our fancy the way small magazines condense big books to suit their readers. And by what we leave out, we distort the parts we let in.

The history of modern nations flows like a stream of corrupted consciousness.

For more than seventy years, Communist ideology slammed the doors of its bureaucratic custodians against reality as it was in Russia. In reality Stalin starved ten million and more of his own countrymen. The system was a morass of corruption and inefficiency; and the stores had no meat, no potatoes, no vegetables, no milk, and no toothpaste for people to buy. But the rulers of Russia looked at all reality through the lenses of Communist dogma. The dogma said that all *must* be well so the leaders said all *was* well.

In the 1930s Lincoln Steffens, a celebrated American journalist, went to Russia to get the truth about Communism during Stalin's most sadistic time. Bernard Baruch, adviser to presidents, asked him, "So you've been over to Russia?" "Yes," replied Steffens, "I have been over to the future, and it works." The bigger the lie, the more eagerly do those who want the lie to be true corrupt their consciousness.

In the same decade two British prime ministers, Stanley Baldwin and Neville Chamberlain, "knew" that Adolf Hitler was a man of peaceful purpose. The House of Commons "knew" that Hitler did not want war. And the reasonable *Times* of London "knew" that Hitler was a reasonable man who could be counted on to do the reasonable thing. But they "knew" it was so only because they so badly wanted it to be so.

Albert Speer, for years Hitler's favorite, told this little story in his memoirs to illustrate the comic idiocy to which Nazi self-deception sank. In 1943 pokey British bombers were suffering a terrible pasting from German fighter planes. In November of that year American fighters began escorting the British bombers. A certain General Galland reported to Field Marshal Goering that American fighter planes had joined the battle for the German skies; they had shot one down, so they knew for sure. Goering screamed, "That's nonsense, Galland, what gives you such fantasies?"

"But sir, they were there!"

"I herewith give you an official order that they were not there. Do you understand? The American fighters were not there."

Then there was the corrupted consciousness that kept America believing that we were winning the Vietnam War until 45,000 Americans were killed, 300,000 American men and women were wounded, over 150 billion dollars were spent, and a beautiful Asian land was left in smoking ruin. Barbara Tuchman writes in her book *The March of Folly:* "At no time were policymakers unaware of the hazards, obstacles, and negative developments. American intelligence was adequate, informed observation flowed steadily from the field to the capital." We knew, but we chose not to know.

The self-deceit practiced by nations is written on a larger scale, but it is no different from the lies we tell ourselves. We do not want to know things that could threaten our investments, subvert our pieties, challenge our prejudices, and in general put too much stress on us. So, in the blink of an eye, we close our minds to reality we do not want to be real.

A mother sees clear signs that her son is on drugs, but closes her eyes; it would hurt too much to know. A husband shuts out clear signals that his wife is having an affair; it would hurt too much to know. Getting older, a teacher closes his mind to signals from students that his lectures are rambling misadventures in boredom; it would hurt too much to know. A famous teacher of theology at a great American seminary lived a notoriously wild and illicit sex life. After he died and the truth was published in a book by his indulgent widow, I asked a colleague of his how it was that nobody at the seminary knew. "We all knew," he said, "and we all refused to know that we knew."

What makes self-deception so hard to overcome is that we never consciously set out to deceive ourselves. A liar may get up in the morning and say, "I am going to lie to my wife today." But nobody ever says, "I think I will lie to myself today." This is the double treachery of self-deception: First we deceive ourselves, and then we convince ourselves that we are not deceiving ourselves.

Reality is flagging us down with red signals, blinking lights, beeping beepers, anything to get our attention. But, in a microsecond, we deny what we know and then we deny that we are denying it. Psychologists call this cognitive dissonance: the experience of having reality we do not want to know bang up against our minds while we deny its existence. "Don't upset me with truth I do not want to know."

Why do we do it? Why bamboozle our own consciousness?

In one sense it is elementary. Reality has gone bad on us. It is loaded with pain and hatred and unfairness and threats and finally death. Reality can be so miserable that no one in his or her right mind wants to know about it.

We Corrupt Our Consciousness When We Are Afraid That Reality Will Rob Us of Our Birthright

I asked an honest white South African why white leaders deceived themselves so badly about the black reality that rapped at their windows. His answer was swift: "We are afraid. We are too scared to know what we know."

Am I any different? Would I have dared to let myself know slavery for the evil it was if I had been a Georgia plantation owner in the year 1850? Would I have dared to know the evil we did to the American Indian had I been staking my own claim on a piece of ground that was their native land? I do not know, but I would not bet a large piece of my pension on my honesty.

Fear is not the only reason we wear blinders.

We Corrupt Our Consciousness When Reality Clashes with Our Faith

Carol Glaubig believed a person who is born again is cleansed of all bad desires. And she knew that her husband, George, was born again. But when they grew up, their two daughters confessed that their father had sexually abused them.

Did their mother know? Yes, they both said, she must have known. But Carol Glaubig said that it never happened. Her husband, George, was born again, and God does not let His reborn children sin. She knew; but to know the truth would threaten her faith, so she refused to know what she knew.

We Corrupt Our Consciousness When Our Passion Blinds Us to What We Know

King David was the apple of God's eye. Everyone, including David, knew it. Now it happened one sultry afternoon that the eye of the apple of God's eye fell on Bathsheba in the beauty of her flesh. And David desired her greatly. She was Uriah's wife, and Uriah was a soldier in David's army. But no matter. When Uriah was off to war, David brought Bathsheba to his royal palace bed and made royal love with her.

Her husband was easy game. "Put Uriah in the front line where the fighting is fiercest," David ordered his general. "Then withdraw from him so he will be struck down and die" (2 Samuel 11:15). Uriah was a goner. David gave Bathsheba a decent time to mourn her husband, and then took her to his bed and board.

The Lord saw it and sent his prophet Nathan to tell David of His deep displeasure. Nathan was not a man to be blunt with a king. So he told David a story about a rich farmer and a poor farmer. The rich farmer had the biggest and best herd of sheep in the country. The poor farmer had a pet lamb and hardly anything else. When the rich man had a dinner party, he took the poor man's lamb and prepared it for his guests.

When he heard the story, David became very angry with the rich farmer. "As surely as the LORD lives, the man who did this deserves to die" (2 Samuel 12:5). David corrupted his consciousness; he would not allow himself to see that he was the rich farmer and that he had stolen from Uriah the lamb of his love. So Nathan made it plain: "You are the man" (verse 7).

The winds of passion blow sand in the eyes of the apples of God's eye.

We Corrupt Our Consciousness When We Are Too Tired to Cope

I do not think I have ever again been as tired as I was during my family's first few weeks in California. We arrived in September. Our first task was to find the right schools for our three children. My second job was to prepare new lectures for a daily eight A.M. class of a hundred students. But during the first week my youngest son was diagnosed with a genetic blood disease. The second week Doris discovered she had cancer. And the third week she had surgery to take it out.

One night, after I had visited Doris at the hospital and tucked the children into bed, I felt too tired to prepare my morning's lecture. I flopped on the bed and leafed through a copy of *Life* magazine. It featured pictures of starving children in Africa. I looked at them for a moment, closed my eyes, and threw the magazine across the room.

"Lord, I'm too tired, I don't want to know."

We can find any number of reasons to fool our own mind. But they all come down to one: our distaste for reality when reality is a bother. The way back to an honest consciousness is the way of courage—courage to look unwanted reality straight in the face. It's the way of hope—hope that we can change reality for the better. And it is the way of gratitude—gratitude for all that is good in spite of the parts that are bad.

THE RIGHT TRUTH AT THE RIGHT TIME

Down in the valley of the Ocklawaha River, where Penny Baxter lived, the men gathered around the stove in the village store on most any Saturday morning in wintertime and did a lot of bragging about their hunting dogs. Everybody expected everybody else to lie about his dog, so it did not really count as lying.

One morning Penny Baxter began running his dog down. "He ain't wuth a good twist o' t'bacey. Sorriest bear dog I ever foller'd." That's the way he went on, grumping about his bear dog, and he got the men quite confused because they weren't used to anybody telling bad truth about his own dog.

"What's go'n on here?" grumped his friend Lemm Forrester. "I never heer'd a man run down his own dog that-a-way." Something fishy here. Must be something special about that dog, and by crooks Lemm meant to get him.

Next day, Lemm came over to Penny's place with a fine shotgun and said he wanted to trade it for the dog. "Naw, you don't want that dog, Lemm, he ain't no good t'all." But Lemm dug in: "Don't argue with me. When I want a dog, I want a dog. Take the gun for him or I'll come and steal him."

Trade made.

Later on, Penny's conscience began pinching him, and he got to feeling guilty about how he had snookered Lemm. But his boy comforted him.

"Shucks, Pa, you told him the truth."

"Yes, Son, my words was straight, but my intention was as crooked as the Ocklawaha River."

Penny Baxter, hero of Marjorie Rawlings's *The Yearling*, knew what truthfulness is about. Honest words match honest intentions. A person has honest intentions when he wants his words to tell somebody what is really on his mind and heart.

Why make such a fuss about words? If reality is ugly, what harm is there in dressing it up a little with words that make reality look better than it is? What's the matter with a little discreet lying, no serious harm meant, just to oil the machinery of effective communication, maybe make a dollar or two?

Some people believe that we should tell the truth for truth's sake. The gossips of our towns tell the truth for truth's sake. They tell everything they know as soon as they hear it, tell it to anyone within earshot, no matter what it is. They use truth like a machete. They slice their way through people and leave them bleeding in the spillage of sacred truth. The bloodshed is sanctified by the sacredness of truth.

I believe that people are the real reason for telling the truth. The apostle Paul said, "Therefore each of you must put off falsehood and speak truthfully to his neighbor, *for we are all members of one body*" (Ephesians 4:25, emphasis added). We owe truthfulness to each other, not for truth's sake, but for each other's sake.

We need to be truthful because every good human relationship is built on communication. And communication rests on trust. When I open my mouth to speak to someone, I make an instant promise that what comes out will speak my mind. And the person who listens to me has a right to trust that my words reveal what is on my mind. In *De mendacio,* Augustine says: "He who tells a lie betrays a trust: for he wishes his listener to put faith in him, while he himself fails to honor that listener's trust."

People who deceive us deny us our right to make

free decisions on the basis of trust. Whether we are deciding to buy a used car, to vote for someone to be president, or to invest in the stock market, we have a right to trust that the salesperson, the candidate, or the broker is telling us what is truly on his or her mind. If they do not tell us the truth as they know it, they deny us our right to make a free decision about reality.

Hypocrisy, sham, cant, phoniness, fraud, humbug, dissimulation, disguise—they are bad because they prevent people from making their own, free, honest response to reality as it is.

One more reason honesty is so important: Lying demeans people. It treats them as if they were not mature enough to be trusted with reality.

"Tell the truth to the British people," Churchill begged the leaders of Britain during the decade of self-deception about Hitler. "They are a tough people, a robust people." But the leaders of the 1930s did not trust people with truth.

During the American presidential campaign of 1964, Lyndon Johnson asked the people to vote for him because he would not expand the war against Vietnam. But Johnson left the campaign trail on weekends, went back to Washington, D.C., and made plans for massive bombing of Hanoi. He demeaned us because he did not deem us mature enough to decide on the basis of the truth.

One night, after a tough day, when family fears were getting close to family reality, Doris asked me why

I had not told her some bad news about one of the children. I said that I thought she had had enough pain, that I did not want to hurt her any more. "Let me decide how much hurt I can stand," she said. "I don't need you to protect me from reality."

But a person of integrity does more than tell people what is on his mind. He learns the art of telling the truth well. To tell it with love—helpfully, healingly, even though painfully—this is the skill that turns honesty into art. This fact takes me back to Aristotle's recipe for honesty with style: the right truth to the right person at the right time in the right way for the right reason.

Let's take a closer look.

The Right Truth

Not every truth I have in my head is mine to tell. A truth confided to me in trust, a truth I promised someone that I would not tell, is not my truth to tell. If my truth will needlessly diminish another or hurt another or tarnish another, it is not my truth to tell.

What is mine to tell? The truth that helps someone who needs it, this is the truth that is mine to tell. The truth another person needs in order to make a free decision, this is the right truth to tell. So is the truth that keeps an intimate relationship honest, or makes a sad person laugh, or reveals a beauty or a mystery that someone may never see if it is not told. And, more than anything, the truth to tell is the truth that another person is loved and forgiven, accepted, beautiful, and worthy.

To the Right Person

A person does not have a right to my truth simply because he asks for it. A friend of mine, call her Janet, told me a deep secret about herself; I promised never to repeat it to another human being. Here is another friend. He asks me: "Is it true that Janet...?"

If I say, "I cannot talk about it," he will guess the truth. If I say, "That is none of your business," I will give the truth away. If I say, "I don't know," I will be lying. But if I tell the truth, I will break my promise. I told the truth. I wish I hadn't.

There are some people to whom we cannot tell the truth because they cannot hear the truth. It enters their ears and is mashed into falsehood as soon as it gets inside their heads. So we *cannot* speak the truth to them. Truth is not only what comes out of our mouths, it is what another person hears.

At the Right Time

You have no obligation to tell a father that your son made Phi Beta Kappa the day his son dropped out of community college. You have no obligation to tell a man about your promotion the day he was fired. You may firmly believe that God has a good purpose in mind when terrible things happen to good people, but the time to tell your truth is not when a mother's child has been killed by a hit-and-run driver.

Some people have an instinct for telling the right truth at the wrong time. But telling it does not make them more honest. Only more cruel. We do well to remember that the apostle Paul himself told us to speak the truth "as fits the occasion" (Ephesians 4:29, RSV).

In the Right Way

It's not just what you say, it's the way you say it. Two teachers told the truth to me once when I was a boy. One of them hurt me with the truth; the other helped me.

It was national hygiene week. Our teacher told each of us to draw a picture to show how we could improve public health. I scrawled a bad cartoon of a man putting the cover on top of a stinking garbage can. She held up the picture for everyone to see, frowned at me, and told the class that mine was an example of how *never* to draw a picture. Could she be the deep reason why I have never even drawn a decent doodle?

The other teacher listened to me give a recitation in front of my class, noticed that I slumped, and that my speech slumped to match my posture. She had a hunch that I was ashamed of being the tallest kid in the class, so she said for my ears only, "Lewis, you have an advantage over the rest of us; be proud of how tall you stand." I have walked erect ever since.

Two surgeons told the same truth to two patients.

One of the surgeons leaned against the doorway as if he wanted to make a quick getaway, told his patient that his tumor was malignant, and left him alone with his horrible truth.

The other surgeon sat down with the patient and his wife and told them a good many things about himself; he talked about his family, how he happened to get into surgery, and what he believed in. One of the things he believed in was the power of hope. Then he asked the patient to tell him a little about his life and about what he believed in. After they had gotten a feel for each other's story, he told his patient that his tumor was malignant, but that he, as a surgeon with years of observing such conditions, was not giving up hope.

For the Right Reason

A truth told for the wrong reason can do more harm than a lie told for the right reason. A lie can be denied and proven false. But a bad truth can only be repeated, exaggerated, and inflated. Telling a truth for a bad reason almost always pays compound interest on pain.

One true word about a senator getting drunk and acting the buffoon in public can corrupt the truth that he had been working to exhaustion on matters of public good and that he is, on the whole, a conscientious and effective senator.

Peter Collier and David Horowitz were working together on a book about the Ford family. They were interviewing Henry Ford II, and getting less than they wanted from him. Ford let them know from the start that he was not going to tell them everything they wanted to know: "There's a lot of stuff you're never going to know about me. And the reason you aren't going to know is not necessarily because I don't want to tell you. But it tears down other people, and that isn't fair."

An artful truth teller uses the truth for a loving reason—to build people up, to encourage them, to help them, to give them a chance to give their own answer to whatever the truth may ask of them.

But Is It a Good Thing to Tell a Lie for a Loving Reason?

André Trocmé was the pastor of the small village of Le Chambon when the Nazis occupied France. He and his wife, Magda, led their whole village to become a city of refuge for runaway Jews during the horrors of the time. After he died the nation of Israel awarded André its highest honor, the Medal of Righteousness. Magda was there to receive it. She heard all the wonderful things said about her husband, and about herself, but she was particularly fascinated by one sentence spoken during the ceremony.

"The righteous are not exempt from evil."

Yes, she thought, they had lied every living day, for three solid years. And perhaps the children of Le Chambon would never again be able to understand how important truth is. But then her back stiffened:

"Ah! Never mind! Jews were running all over the place after a while, and we had to help them quickly. We had to help them—or let them die, perhaps—and in order to help them, unfortunately we had to lie."

And yet, and yet, and yet. Can anyone keep on lying for any loving reason without eventually clouding the eye?

Tom Sawyer's schoolmaster whipped his pupils for every minor misdemeanor he could catch them at. Becky Thatcher tore out a page from the schoolmaster's favorite book. A major misdemeanor, and she was in for it.

Tom felt a mighty affection for Becky. So when the master asked the guilty person to confess, Tom stood up and, without a glance at Becky, said that he had done it and was ready for whipping. He got it.

Becky told her father how Tom had taken the whipping for her at school. Her father was a judge and was used to making judicious pronouncements about guilt and innocence. As for Tom's lie, he declared, "It was a noble, a generous, magnanimous lie—a lie that was worthy to hold up its head and march down through history breast to breast with George Washington's lauded Truth about the hatchet."

Becky thought her father had never looked so tall and so superb as when he walked the floor and stamped his foot and spoke such a blessing on Tom Sawyer's lie. If I were in her shoes, I would have admired my father for blessing Tom's lie just as she did.

But in the crooked ways of the world, too many gallant lies lead us gently into a moral mush where lying is fine whenever it saves us a little trouble. Telling one loving lie does not turn a person of integrity into a liar any more than one wrong note turns a concert violinist into a barn-dance fiddler. But if you get used to getting away with a wrong note, you may get careless with yourself, and become just another fiddler when you could have been an artist.

⌁ ⌁

I have tried to say in this chapter that integrity is about holding our lives together so that we are the same person inside and out, backward and forward. We create integrity as we own whatever story we are called on to write by the living of our lives. If we begin by owning our own stories in truth, we are ready to own reality and resist the corruption of our consciousness. And when we are able to own reality for what it is, we are ready to speak our minds with honesty and love.

Integrity is not an optional part of ourselves. A good car can lack air-conditioning and still be a splendid automobile. But if we lack integrity, we lose our hold on the other components that go into the making of a pretty good person. Losing integrity is more like having our lungs cave in; everything else goes out with them.

No living person has yet arrived whole at the place called integrity. If anyone tells you that he is a person of integrity, get a second opinion. We do well just to keep moving in the right direction. We have to check on our own intentions regularly, and see whether we are still moving on the journey or whether, at some shadowed station, we left the train and went off to nowhere. For, without integrity, anywhere is nowhere.

CHAPTER 4

Taking Charge of Our Lives

Early on, he didn't know exactly when, Larry Den Besten had a hunch that he was here in the world to heal people. Maybe healing their bodies in medicine, maybe their souls in the church, maybe both. So he covered his bets and studied both theology and medicine. He earned a degree in theology, then one in medicine, and the day after he finished his last medical exam he left for Nigeria.

Once he had gotten a working knowledge of Hausa, a tribal tongue of northern Nigeria, he planned and built a small hospital from the ground up in a village called Mkar. For the next decade he spent most of his waking hours in its whitewashed, bare-walled operating room. He stood on his feet ten or twelve hours a day, six days a week, hunching over the bodies of people who suffered from almost every conceivable malignancy, improvising new slices and stitches as he went. Some evenings, after operating on people for ten hours straight, he would get into a Piper Cub and fly a couple of hundred miles into the bush to take care of one or another old person too sick to make her or his way to the hospital.

But he did not intend to write his whole story

in Africa. He worked there for ten years, then came home. Eventually he joined the medical center of the University of California in Los Angeles as a surgeon and teacher of surgery. Around the surgical units he earned the nickname "Quick Fingers Den Besten" because nobody else could operate with his speed. And swiftness mattered a great deal when it came to building an entire new esophagus out of a patient's intestines, the sophisticated sort of operation that added extra sheen to his rising star.

He was determined, however, not to be a captive of his own success. So, after ten years, he took the whole package in his hands—with its prestige and money and all the other perks that successful surgeons enjoy—looked at it hard, and set it all aside. (Some people said he threw it all away.) This time he bewildered his medical fraternity by choosing to become, of all things, the hands-on director—the provost—of a graduate school of theology, Fuller Seminary, where I work.

Less than three years into the seminary chapter, he did lose control: to chronic pain, to enervating cramps, to mistaken diagnoses, to cancer, and finally to death.

He used to say, after years of watching people live and die, that people tended to die the way they lived. It was true of him. He died the way he lived, fighting for control.

His cancer-shot body would beg him to go home and rest, but he did not want to lose control yet. So he swallowed some pills and stuck around the office.

When he finally did leave for the day, he would pull his old surgeon's smock and his leather doctor's bag out of his closet, plod on over to a mission a couple of blocks away, and tend to the medical needs of the homeless people who hung out around there.

But he did lose control, and he did die.

THE DIRECTION WE WANT TO TAKE

I thought Larry Den Besten overdid control; he held the reins too tightly for me. Good friend that he was, I was never completely relaxed with him. I feel more comfortable with people who show some weakness, kick up their heels, let out a head of steam, and do something a little crazy now and then. So I do not mean to parade Larry across our stage so that we can judge ourselves by his example.

I told you about Larry Den Besten because I think his life tells us what self-control is really about.

First, self-control is about deciding for ourselves the direction we want our story to take. It is about writing the kind of story with our lives that we think we are meant to write, not the story somebody else wants us to write.

Second, self-control is about being in harmony with ourselves. It is about knowing who we are and what we are about. "Identity" is the fashionable word for what I am talking about.

And third, self-control means keeping on top of the rambunctious passions inside of us. This is, to be sure, a narrow sense of self-control. But very important as a means to an end. The end is to steer our lives in the direction we really want them to take, keeping close to who we really are all the while. To achieve our end, we need to prevent our passions from taking over.

Let's poke about in these three thoughts.

First, deciding on our own direction in life: Self-controlled people write their own stories, conceive their own plot, decide when it's time to wrap up a chapter and begin a new one. If we have self-control, we don't tailor our stories to fit somebody else's plot. We don't write our stories to fit the script dictated by others—our favorite teacher maybe, or even our parents. People with self-control write their own stories.

Second, keeping some sameness within ourselves: People with self-control can wrap up one chapter of their story, go on to the next, maybe in a different place or at a different job, and stay the same basic person all through the different chapters. Holding on to who and what we really are while we pass through all the changes of our life, this is the mark of self-control.

Oh yes, we grow, we adapt, we take on new styles, maybe get converted a few times—and yet we are the same person no matter how many years we live or how many different things we do. This was true of Larry: I knew him early on, and I knew him in his dying, and there was a core at the center of him that I could always identify as the real Larry Den Besten.

If we cannot keep our identity through all the stages of our lives, we are torn in pieces. Yes, I am complex; sometimes I feel like two or three different people. But being a complex person is different from being several people, the way an orchestra is different from a collection of musicians.

Now the third thing about self-control: It is, in fact, a lot like conducting an orchestra. There are some powerful players down there inside of me—passions, desires, angers, sex drives, terrors of memories past and threats to come, and a lot more. My job is to set them free to play their parts. But if I let any one of them take charge, I would not have an orchestra; what I would have is a bunch of soloists on a binge.

Being a maestro in control of the orchestra is about playing beautiful music. It is not about enjoying the power; it is not about strutting our stuff in front of an audience. It is about making the kind of music the orchestra enjoys playing—and the rest of us enjoy hearing.

Self-control is important for the same reason that it's important for a pilot to be in control of a commercial airliner: not to show off his skills at controlling that huge flying machine, but to get his passengers home in one piece.

Let's try one more illustration.

Imagine a troupe of prima donnas on stage for the first rehearsal of a new play. Everybody is out to get the best lines, dictate the tempo, and bend the whole script his or her way. The rehearsal is about to become a scramble for control.

Then the director walks on stage. She knows the story and what the author meant by it, and she has a clear sense of how to transform the cold script into living theater. She respects the talents of the old troopers and the young hopefuls. She takes control of them out of respect for them. And, precisely by controlling what they do, she sets them free to play their parts to the hilt. And together they bring it off on opening night.

The point again: The director is not there to enjoy being the boss; she is there to help the players create something fantastic.

What Hamlet said to his group of actors could be aimed at the players that strut and bellow inside of us: "In the very torrent, tempest, and—as I may say—whirlwind of passion, you must acquire and beget a temperance."

Ah, "temperance," the classic way of saying self-control: Beget a temperance so that you can write a fine story with your life.

Life gets to be a mess without it. Take the lowly sphincter muscle as a vulgar parable. Getting control of the sphincter muscle is one of the five-star moments in a child's growing up. Lose it in your old age and you've got a nasty metaphor for the loss of self-control.

The book of Proverbs states, "Like a city whose walls are broken down is a man who lacks self-control"

(25:28). No wonder the Bible teaches us that self-control is the backbone of the good life. No wonder either that Aristotle said that self-control is a staple in living a "fine and noble" life.

WE CAN BE IN CHARGE

Conrad, the likable lad we meet in Judith Guest's *Ordinary People*, feels as if somebody else or something else has taken charge of his life. For one thing, he is obsessed with a horrible memory. His older brother—who, everyone said, was a lot smarter and more popular than Conrad—drowned when their boat capsized. Conrad hung on to the hull; the brother tried to swim to shore; he never made it. Now Conrad is sure that his mother wishes that he had died instead of his brother. He feels that way himself most of the time, and the guilt of it has a choke hold on him.

Here he is, on his first visit with a rumpled psychiatrist named Berger:

"So what're you doing here? You look like a healthy kid to me."

"I'd like to be more in control, I guess."

"Well, okay. I'd better tell you. I'm not big on control. I prefer things fluid. In motion."

[But he takes Conrad on as a patient and tells him that he ought to come twice a week.]

"Twice a week?"

"Control is a tough nut."

How well I know. Nobody knows better than I

do how hard it is to be in charge of our own life. Obviously, I cannot be everything I may take it into my head to be. I cannot be a relief pitcher for the Dodgers or an astronaut headed for the moon. I will never be a Mother Teresa, either; certainly never a Jesus of Nazareth. There are limits. But it's a tough nut even when you are dealing with fundamentals.

I sometimes wonder, in fact, if I'm destined forever to be a clone of my mother. After all the time I've had to become a somebody of my own, I am still stuck with some of the same quirks she had. Take the way she would repent when she bought something expensive for herself. She bought a secondhand Roper once, our very first gas stove, to take the place of the old coal burner that warmed us to the bones in the kitchen. A major move. For two weeks she got herself up in the middle of the night, brooded at the kitchen table, head in hands, eyes fixed on the cold white Roper, mourning her spendthrift folly.

We thought she was a little crazy in this regard. But here I am, more than a half-century later, incurably afflicted with the same weakness. I bought a new car once, a Toyota Cressida. And by the time I had driven it home I knew for sure it was the wrong car for me—too big, too expensive. I knew for sure that God would strike me dead—what about all the poor people who had no car at all? Two days later I was back at the dealer's showroom, trying to persuade the salesman to take it back. He had been like an uncle, wanted to do nothing but good for me when he sold it to me, but now he talked like a mocking stranger: "Look mister, the minute you drove that car out of here what you were driving was a used car."

A tough nut, taking charge of your life when you've got a parent inside of you calling the shots.

And yet nothing anyone has said about psychic conditioning or genetic fate has convinced me that I am only a pawn in a chess game that someone else is playing.

I talked earlier about how we have to own the raw materials we were stuck with before we have a chance to begin our story. The raw material some of us were handed—the psychic whammies our parents put on us and the genetic blueprint they sneaked inside of us—may put us at a disadvantage. But it's the only raw material we are ever going to have.

Now I want to say that we have the power to take the same raw materials into ourselves and write a good story with them no matter how unpromising they were. We can write our own story, the one we were meant to write, the story nobody else should ever write for us.

For starters, I can put one foot ahead of the other, point it, and order the other leg to follow. This is something nobody should sneeze at. When we decide to move our feet in a path we choose to walk, and when our feet do what our mind tells them to do, we are performing a small human miracle.

I like the way psychologist Rollo May defines the human will in his book *Love and Will:* "Will is the capacity to organize one's self so that movement in a certain direction or toward a certain goal can take place." An inner power to organize the different parts of ourselves—our drives, our passions, our hankerings, our dreams, our hopes—to organize them to move together in the direction we intend to take; this is the power that makes our planned movements so critically different from the buzzing of a fly or even the frolicking of a dolphin.

But we have another power with longer range. We call it *intention.* We have an intention when we get a fix on a future goal, a program we plan to pursue, a job we set ourselves to finish.

The importance of having an intention became real to me one cold morning when I wanted to stay in bed a lot more than I wanted to do anything else.

The cold has crept through the bedroom window on gopher's paws. It is ten degrees below zero outside, a draft blows through the open window and brushes my cheeks. Sprays of snow have blown in and lie on the bare hardwood floor; they do not melt.

Below my chin, my body is nestled along

the supple undulations of my partner's form. The womb is wonderful. My flesh and my soul cry out in me: Stay where you are!

But at seven o'clock I feel a nudge from inside my bedded psyche. It dumps me feet first on the cold oak floor. I put on the sort of mesh underwear that a sunbelt senior citizen wears in a real man's winter, mumble through hot oatmeal and coffee, pull on my boots, and kick a path to my windowless room in the basement of the library at St. John's University in Collegeville, Minnesota.

How did it happen? How did my weak will win out against my strong desire?

The pioneer of American psychology, William James, would have said that my weakish will to get up caught my strong desire to sleep off guard, the way a crafty old fighter catches his younger opponent blinking and knocks him down with a swift left hook. In the same way my will saw my desire blink, sneaked in a jab, and knocked me out of bed.

Maybe.

But I think something else was getting its way with me. I came to Minnesota with an intention. I intended to write a book. And my long-term intention to write that book took a lease on my mind, and at the critical moment my intention prevailed over my short-term desire to stay in bed. My will was partner with my intention and together they got me going.

DEALING WITH TAKEOVER BIDS

We are shadowed by four forces that want to take over our lives. One is a friendly force; the second is a necessary force; the third is a passive force; and then, fourthly, there are downright hostile forces. We can lose control to them one at a time, or all at once. Let's review the four takeover threats.

The Friendly Takeover: Desire

Desire is a good friend. It lights fires in our bellies. It makes us itch for what we've never had enough of, hunger for something better than we've ever tasted, thirst for living waters we've never drunk. Desire adds imagination to our wills and heat to our intentions. T. S. Eliot said, "God exults when a [person] comes through with a wish of his own," and I think he was right.

But we need to control desire for the same reason we need to control a thoroughbred. If you want an exciting run for your money, you need the thoroughbred's desire; but if you don't control him you'll never win a race. A person with no desire plods the same route every day, like a working nag. And who wants to be a sparkless plug? Lose the desire, and we lose the fun of living.

But, out of control, desire is trouble.

The risky thing about any desire is that it can heat up into an addiction.

Smoking cigarettes was the toughest addiction I have ever had to break. At midnight, after I had smoked too much, I "knew" I was in control of cigarettes, and I had it in me to stop the very next morning. But the next morning before I took a third swallow of coffee, I lit up and took the day's first of a couple hundred drags. One morning, when I knew I was hooked for another day, I told Doris, "If I had to choose between you and cigarettes, I think I would choose cigarettes." She was smart enough to recognize my sick humor for a confession that I was hooked, and that I needed the help I finally sought.

We all have our addictions—money, power, sex, anything. Some of them we can make peace with; if you're addicted to jogging or eating creamed herring before going to bed, there's not much reason to worry. But other addictions grab the steering wheel of our lives and prevent us from going in the direction we really want to go. These are the ones we need to resist.

Tradition offers us two simple solutions to addiction.

One is the old-fashioned moral solution: *Buckle up your will and quit.* Let a drunk or a junkie just use his God-given willpower. And that is all there is to it. Damningly simple.

The other is the old-fashioned medical solution: *Addicts need curing the same way cancer patients do.*

Addiction is a sickness. Some people get it and some don't. And that's all there is to it. Demeaningly simple.

The moral solution does not take human tragedy seriously; it does not take account of the fact that we are sometimes victims of forces beyond our control. The medical solution does not take human responsibility seriously; it relieves people too quickly of the hallmark of their humanity, personal accountability.

Can we find our way beyond these shortsighted views of how we lose control and how to get it back again?

The best wisdom suggests that many of us go through three phases on our way into and out of addiction.

First phase: We freely do something that gives us pleasure. Since it gives us instant pleasure, we choose to do it again. And again. And again.

Second phase: We lose our power to say no to the desire. We are caught—maybe very quickly, maybe after years. Either way, however, we are out of control.

Third phase: We admit to ourselves that we have lost control and that we cannot get it back again on our own. We face up to the fact that we are shackled. And when we've suffered too much, we seek help in our helplessness.

The trip back to control is a long and painful journey, too long and too painful for some to finish. But the people who get there are usually the ones who surrender to the truth that they had lost their way.

Desire is a good friend; life is flat and flaccid without it. Apathy is no virtue. But desire is a friend that will take over control of our lives if we let it.

The Second Takeover Bid: Anger, a Necessary but Dangerous Source of Energy

What a gift anger is! The adrenaline flows, the heart gallops, the blood pressure takes off, and we are ready to fly into action, like a jay in defense of her nested jaylets. Anger mobilizes our energies to fight back.

Anger is to our personal lives what the military is to national life. Given the state of the world, a nation needs the military. But let the military establishment take over, and a nation will lose control of itself. So it is with anger. A person without anger is a pushover. But anger on its own is a tyrant.

For one thing, anger—like desire—has no controls of its own; it flames until the fuel is spent and people lie burned in its path. A mother whose anger is under control disciplines her child; a mother whose anger is out of control abuses her child. A driver in control of his anger utters a mild obscenity at a driver who cuts in front of him on the freeway; an angry driver out of control runs him off the road.

For another thing, anger is blind. "Blind wrath," wrote philosopher Josef Pieper, "shuts the eyes of the spirit before they have been able to grasp the facts and to judge them." It cannot see the difference between things we *ought* to fight against and things we can put up with.

Is anger always a demonic fury whirling out of

control in the underworld of our spirits? Or can we, as the Bible says, get angry and sin not?

A friend of mine tells me that his seventeen-year-old daughter gets him mad enough to wring her neck. But she does not get him angry. He gets himself angry. She knows the buttons to push, but he gives her control of the buttons.

He can predict the sorts of situations that trigger his rage. He sees the signals of a coming eruption the way a farmer in Oklahoma can see a tornado on its way to town. And, if he keeps his wits about him, he can steer his way around the situation like a pilot who flies around turbulence.

Anger is not always turbulence. Sometimes anger is a mole that burrows beneath the surface. It takes control by stealth. We do not even know what it is we are angry about. It could be our loveless father, or our manipulative mother, or it could be God. But unless we do find out who or what we are angry at, we hand control over to an underground rage with a hundred disguises.

I have talked about losing control to two powerful passions, desire and anger. But there is a third force that can take control without any passion at all. No rage. No ecstasy. Just an apathy that slides us straight into control by conformity.

The Third Takeover Bid: Conformity

Conformists look like the very models of control. They never eat too much, never drink too much, never dress up in any outlandish colors. They are correct in every detail, orderly, efficient, careful, scrupulous; no excess in sight. They escape the snares of passion, but they fall mindlessly into convention.

They read the books that book clubs decide they shall read. They see the movies that the Hollywood hypsters tell them they should see. They vote the way the pollsters tell them other people vote. From cradle to grave they give their lives over to the crowd, to convention, to conformity.

What liberates conformists is the discovery of unconditional love. If they ever discover a love that has no strings attached, no need to earn it, they also discover that they can go out on a limb, fall off, and still be fine. When conformists let someone love them unconditionally, they dare again to risk taking responsibility for the direction of their own lives.

The Hostile Takeover

In Carl Junction, Missouri, almost everybody in town goes to a Bible-believing church and tries to live the Bible's way. But, as reported in the *Los Angeles Times* on October 20, 1988, even in such a town things can go wrong. For it was in the quiet town of Carl Junction, after church one Sunday, that three boys clubbed a friend to death with baseball bats—for the fun of it.

Jim Hardy said the devil made them do it.

Jim was the leader of the group. Steve Newberry was an outsider who wanted too much to be an insider.

The boys were often stoned on dope, listened to a lot of heavy metal rock music, and secretly devoted themselves to Satan. Jim recalled that Satan had made a promise to him: "Just open the door once and I promise I'll never let you go." He opened the door. And lost control.

He and his friends found their best fun by killing people's cats and dogs. But torturing animals went flat on them; they felt a craving to up the ante. On a sunny Sunday, smoking pot with his two friends and Steve, Jim heard a voice inside his head telling him:

"Do it now."

He clubbed Steve on the head with a baseball bat. Steve fell, got up and tried to run away, but fell down.

"Why me?" he whimpered.

"Because it's fun, Steve."

They clubbed him again and again until he was dead. When it was over, Jim said, "Sacrifice to Satan."

Could it be true? Could Jim Hardy have been possessed by Satan? We will not take his word for it. But it is true that if we play too many games with evil, we are eventually controlled by evil.

Suppose that, at a forgotten but critical moment, Jim Hardy made a decision not to resist evil. And suppose that his decision not to resist was actually a surrender to forces that took control of him at the center.

Some experts are sure that they can tell if a person is possessed. Here is how psychiatrist M. Scott Peck, in his book *People of the Lie,* describes a person possessed by a demon:

> When the demonic finally spoke clearly in one case, an expression appeared on the patient's face that could be described only as Satanic. It was an incredibly contemptuous grin of utter hostile malevolence.... The eyes were hooded with lazy, reptilian torpor...open wide with blazing hatred.

But the demonic need not be spectacular. Many sober Germans gave their lives over to the demonic with a bland banality. Hannah Arendt watched Adolf Eichmann—the master engineer of the Holocaust—while he was on trial in Jerusalem. She saw him not as a monster, but as a blank, dull, commonplace clerk of a man who had given himself over to evil unlimited. Uncommon evil finds its niche in common conformity.

How did Eichmann lose control? In teaspoons. Each of Eichmann's early choices was piddling: joining the party, accepting assignments, getting promotions, wheedling his way into bureaucratic favor. But each choice was a link in the chain that lashed his petty life to inhuman evil.

What makes takeover a real threat to ordinary people is that we are seldom enticed to bargain away our souls, like Faust, in a single seduction. Evil whittles away, slicing a sliver here and a shaving there, getting us into the habit of making measly little compromises with deceit until we have vacated our control center and handed it over to the lie.

Satan is no fool. Getting a poor devil to roll his eyes and make a gargoyle of his face is not a demonic triumph. Get an ordinary person committed sober-faced to an uplifting, inspiring lie, however, and you have gotten yourself a prize—if you happen to be a demon.

In sum, when it comes to being possessed, ask not whether you have been slightly loony; ask rather whether lying has become your lifestyle.

GETTING FREE TO FIND OUR OWN WAY

Self-control is about being in charge of the direction our lives are taking.

Now for the paradox: We get control of our lives, ultimately, not by willpower but by surrender. The final secret lies in amazing grace. This is the surprise of all surprises on anybody's journey: On the last stretch we ride home free.

Here are some pathways into the freedom we desire.

Finding Our Families

Everyone needs what Erik Erikson calls a "persistent sameness within one's self." We need an identity to know who we are and what our stories are about. But we write our stories in a certain setting. And we have to keep in touch with our setting. For this we need to be part of a group of people who are committed to us. Erik Erikson again: To get a persistent sameness we need a "persistent sharing with others."

Enter the family—the home haven of persistent sharing. A family is an intimate circle of people who are committed to "persistent sharing" of each other. It is commitment, not blood, that creates the family; there are five people in my immediate family, and not one of us has a blood relationship with any other. But we *are* a family because we are committed.

No matter how far away we move from our first family, we have to hold onto a lifeline that leads back to it. The lifeline is memory. The memory of our family is our umbilical cord back to that original "persistent sharing" out of which we grow into the "sameness within ourselves" that tells us who we really are.

So we all find ways to keep alive the memories that nourish us. One winter Saturday a couple of my nephews sat down with my mother and got her talking about the days before they were born. She told them about a grandmother who refused to be put to sleep during surgery because, if she was going to heaven, she wanted to be awake for the trip. She told them how my grandfather required my father to walk ten miles each way to get to a school in the next village, where they would teach him in the Bible's way. She told about the hungry days and lonely seasons of settling as strangers in a new country, and about the dreams that never did come true. She told the stories, and the nephews put them on tape so that all her children's children can share a tribal memory.

Before they are allowed to collect social security, every parent and grandparent alive should be required to sit down with their children and record their memories of the olden days. The tapes should be played at every birthday—the tribal storytellers telling the stories of their family's earlier days so that a child can have a family memory.

Some people's lifeline gets so clogged with bitterness that they can suck no nourishment through it. They wander all their lives looking for a new family where they can become a somebody in persistent sharing with other somebodies.

Liesel Brooks was only a little eleven-year-old girl living in a little German town, when one day she accidentally learned that her parents had been Nazis. Her father was already dead then, and her mother reared her in silence about the past. But now she knew. As reported in the *Los Angeles Times,* on October 26, 1988, "Suddenly, I knew that my parents, specifically my father, had been Nazis. I faced my mother and shouted, 'You are murderers! Don't ever touch me again!' "

From that early time Liesel was a stranger in her own setting. Home was a frozen scene of mother-daughter resentment. Finally, when the mother sent her rebel away to a boarding school, Liesel left and never came home again.

She went to England and wandered there, an alien,

for twenty years. Then she came to the United States—still, in her own words, "a rootless, stateless wanderer, holding on to layer upon layer of hurt and guilt." She lied about her beginnings to everyone, even to her two ex-husbands.

Then she surrendered to the truth that we cannot find a persistent sameness within ourselves if we cannot let ourselves have a memory.

"It came to me gradually and painfully that if you do not like where you come from, you do not like yourself. I knew that I had to break that vicious circle."

She found a substitute family, a support group in Los Angeles, and there she met a Jewish woman named Rachel. Rachel was rejecting her own story's setting for reasons ironically different from Liesel's. She was ashamed of her family because they had *survived* the Holocaust. But Rachel came to love her parents for what they were, survivors, through no fault or no credit of their own. And thus she accepted her memory and found herself again.

Rachel gave Liesel freedom to remember the truth.

"I began sobbing in front of all these strangers. I revealed that my parents had been loyal supporters of Adolf Hitler."

Her confession was the first stage of her forgiving. In the power of forgiving, she began to accept—not to approve of, but to accept—her family and own it as the raw material for her life story.

Some people find an extended family through

their faith. I am one of them. Now and then, when my faith is primed, I chew a piece of bread and sip a nip of wine in Holy Communion to reopen my memory life-line to an immense family.

It doesn't happen every time, but now and then I feel as if the ancient Jews become my family. The apostles and martyrs become my family. The Orthodox in Russia become my family. The Catholics in Poland and the Pentecostals in Chile become my family. The wretched of the earth become my family. And remembering that I belong to this spiritual family helps me know who I am and where I fit.

Getting Control by Letting Go

For every person who loses control to his or her rambunctious passions, there are a hundred who lose control to the unfair wounds they did not deserve to feel.

Someone they trusted betrayed them. Someone they loved brutalized them. Someone they depended on left them dangling alone. They are deeply hurt. But it is not only the hurt that they remember. It is the feeling of outrage at being wronged.

Hurt and wronged, the memory is like a videotape permanently installed in our minds. We cannot turn it on; we cannot turn it off. We are condemned to let it play its wretched reruns inside our minds at its own whim. Our bitter memory of wrongful pain takes control.

Why do we hang on to it? For one reason, nothing

on earth makes us feel more virtuous than remembered wrongs. Or gives us such perverse pleasure. Homer, the ancient Greek poet, noticed how it "rises within our soul and becomes in our madness a thing more sweet than the dripping of honey." Hate is the soul's cocaine; it gives us a sweet high, but sooner or later it brings us low.

The only way back to control over our painful memories is the way of forgiveness. When we forgive we surrender our basic human right to get even with the person who hurt us. But this surrender is not a defeat. It is the ultimate win.

When we forgive an ancient wrong, we set a prisoner free and discover that the prisoner we set free is us. When we forgive, we dance again to the melody of healing. When we forgive, we reclaim control of our lives from the slavery of a hurting memory.

Surrendering

One almost certain way to lose control is to deliver our lives over to other people's approval.

Life becomes a slavish scramble to win the approval of someone very important to us. We write our stories to get their approval; we do the writing, but they dictate the plot. We always fail.

One reason we fail is that we never get enough approval to satisfy us; every pat on the back leaves us needing more the next time.

The chase becomes very depressing. Hot pursuit of approval leads us finally into despair. The time comes when we get too tired for the hunt; we submit to the sneaking hunch inside of us that we are not good enough for anyone to approve of us, not anyone who matters to us—not mother, not father, not God. When we get to this point, we sink into a minor—or, sometimes, a major—depression. It is a loss of control.

I have intimate acquaintance with the experience.

I had been hunting for approval all my life. I wanted most of all to get my mother to approve of me. Close behind her was God. I could never keep the difference between them clear. In any case getting Mother's nod was the theme of my story. But finally I knew for sure that my story would never be good enough for her.

Her name was Rena Benedictus. She was a Frisian farm girl who fell into true love with Melle Smedes, a dreamer of a Frisian blacksmith. She married him and followed him to the United States, to a small village called Reeman buried in western Michigan, where other Frisians had gone before and where he was sure good things waited for them. He took over a blacksmith shop in a village of five or six horses, and failed. He tried farming for a while and failed at that too. He invented a carbide lighting system for farming people, and took out a patent on it; but electricity came to the country before carbide had a chance.

He moved his family—five of them now; I was yet to come—to Muskegon, a rising industrial town. There he took a grinding job at one of its foundries and built a house for his family at night, after work. At age thirty-one he was as tired and wasted as an old man. One morning, before the house was finished, he fell back into bed as he got up for work and died of heart failure.

Rena had no family. She had no job skills. She spoke a mix of English and Frisian. So, a week after Rena buried her husband, she began scrubbing other people's floors and washing their clothes in a cranky secondhand Maytag.

She usually left home before we left for school and got home a couple of hours after we did. We were early latchkey kids, only there was no key because we had no latch. One morning, a half hour or so after she left the house, I was shuffling my way to school down Apple Street when I drew near a frame house with a small cement porch. As I got closer I saw her, on her hands and knees, scrubbing that preposterous stoop. I had never actually seen what she did when she was away from home, and now I saw her, head toward the door, round back end facing me, in this humble posture. I was a half-baked fourth grader, and I wanted to slink by without her seeing me. But just as I approached she happened to rise to her knees; she pushed her loose hair back from her face and turned her head in my direction. We looked at each other for an eternal moment.

"Halo Lewis," she said. Her voice told me she was embarrassed for me. I was embarrassed for her. I turned my head toward her and muttered a weak, "Hi." Then I looked away. I was ashamed, and she knew.

Once a month she walked to the stately red brick courthouse that sat in the middle of a grassy square near the center of town. There she picked up the eight dollars that the county fathers provided for its needy widows—a dollar and a quarter a month for each of us. Sometimes she took me with her. But when we got near the courthouse I lagged a few steps behind. I was ashamed of her.

All my life I have been shadowed by shame for having been ashamed of her. And I have devoted a large section of my life to proving that I was not ashamed of her after all and that she did not have to be ashamed of me. Earning her blessing was my life's work, but I never could earn it. I had once been ashamed of a great woman. She was forever too good for me. I could never, never hear her say: "This is my son, in whom I am well pleased."

Besides, she did not have enough confidence in herself to approve of me. She could not approve of herself. How could she approve of me?

And so the impossibility of earning her approval became my life's despair. I lost control of my own story; I lost it to my need for an approval I could never get and she could never give. I was destined to depression.

I was also sick of being depressed, sick enough to seek a crash assault on my own sickness. I knew a certain John Finch, up in the coastal village of Gig

Harbor, Washington, and I knew his reputation for helping people like me by means of an intensive three-week session of therapy. The intensity of his approach terrified me. It would expose me to the core of my life; everything I was ashamed of would be laid bare and I feared I could not bear the baring of my soul.

My fear was the final test of my sincerity. So I called him. He invited me to come up. I went.

In another book *How Can It Be All Right When Everything Is All Wrong?* I told the story of what happened to me there. But it is so crucial to the point of this chapter that I need to tell it again. I spent three weeks alone in a cabin on Fox Island in Puget Sound, a long bridge away from Gig Harbor. There I holed up without a television set or a radio, without a newspaper, without the use of a telephone, and without a book to read. And I was also without people, except for a regular six A.M. visit with John Finch.

My task was to do nothing for three weeks but to carry on an imaginary conversation with my mother and to keep a journal of my feelings about our conversation. It felt silly, but I did it anyway. I talked with her for two weeks and, as we talked, I descended ever more deeply into my feelings of helplessness. My cure was far worse than my disease.

Midafternoon, on a soft Indian summer day, I reached my crisis. I was pacing a short stretch of frayed carpet, making a circular path around a few sticks of straight-backed furniture, back and forth, bent like a crooked old man, feeling with every orbit a new terror at being absolutely out of control of my life.

I felt alone, dangling over the edge, falling where nobody could rescue me with the good news that I was good enough for them to approve of me. It was all inward, of course, a spiritual experience. It was my free fall into the dark night of my soul. I was lost for want of Mother's good pleasure. I fell into my own abyss.

And I fell into the hands of God.

The scaffolding of other people's approval collapsed, but I was held. I experienced the moment of despair and discovery that a Jewish poet wrote about in Psalm 139:8,10: "If I make my bed in hell, behold, thou art there...even there...thy right hand shall hold me" (KJV). I made my bed in my hell and his hand held me. I was not in control and still I was safe.

I went for a walk, and while I walked God talked to me—or I imagined he did—which was odd because I do not ordinarily hear the voice of God. He said to me: "You will never need to earn anyone's approval. Not even mine. You will survive without it." I said aloud, which was even more out of character for me, "Do you mean that, Lord?" And he seemed to say, "Yes, I do."

It was not an abiding cure for all my problems, not by a long shot. I backslide often. If it isn't Mother's approval I seek, it's somebody else's. But it's never the way it was before.

I think I discovered for myself the deepest paradox

of self-control. It is this: One way to get in control of one's life is surrender to unconditional love. The love that accepts me with no reference to my deserving. I have to get back to that surrender now and then or I lose control again to the demon of other people's approval.

PRACTICING CONTROL

There is only one way to stay in control of anything. How did Isaac Stern get control over Brahms's violin concerto? How did Orel Hersheiser learn to control a slider so well that he got it over the edge of the plate more often than he missed it? How did Kareem Abdul Jabbar get to control his sky hook? Everlasting repetition. Practice!

"Keep the faculty of effort alive in you by a little gratuitous exercise every day so that when the hour of dire need draws nigh, it may find you not unnerved and untrained to stand the test"—the counsel of William James. Gratuitous exercise is like practicing your speech *before* you interview for a job. Let's think of some gratuitous exercises that could help us regain and keep control of our life stories.

The Practice of Intention

We can disengage ourselves from the world around us once every day by spending five minutes alone, undistracted, in silent thought about what we intend to do with our lives. Where do we want to go? What do we plan for the next two years? What sort of story do we want to write?

By asking about our intentions, we may discover we have some already. And putting our intentions into words may give us a boost on the way to carrying them out. It is like renewing commitments; repeating them aloud creates an energy for keeping them.

The Practice of Memory

One way to draw strength from our family is simply to seize a few minutes every day to relive our childhood. Try to recall a story your father or mother told you about their childhoods; search for moments when your father or mother let you know that they would be on your side, no matter what. Let yourself go back to the places you played, the rooms you slept in, the classrooms of the schools you went to, the secret places you found to hide away in. Let your best memories settle in your mind.

I practice by thinking about the picnics my mother made for us on the Fourth of July. She was an immigrant, not even a citizen, and she couldn't write an English sentence—but she knew how to celebrate the Fourth. She would get up early to mix a batch of potato salad and make bologna and peanut butter sandwiches, enough of them to fill the six of us at two meals. Then she'd add twelve bananas (two for each of us, one for lunch and the other for supper) and a couple of mason jars filled with lemonade, and she'd stack it all into two of the finer picnic baskets ever lugged to a county park.

About ten in the morning the six of us would set out on foot together up Getty Street a couple of miles north. We'd walk single file (because Getty was a main artery and had no sidewalks) down through the celery farm basin and up again until we came to Marquette Street, the starting point for a trolley car that took us to the rolling white sand dunes on the shore of Lake Michigan. By the time we got there and found ourselves a vacant spot to spread out on, we were ready to eat. My memories of those picnic lunches still signal to my heart that the world is too good a place not to have a fine future.

About two in the afternoon a crew of men appeared mysteriously on the beach to ready things for the annual Fourth of July balloon ascension. The crew spread a menacing black canvas over the beach. One of the men crawled beneath it, set a gas blower at the very center, and turned it on, so that its breath slowly blew that dead mass of tarpaulin into a mammoth, lighter-than-air balloon. As soon as the canvas began to inflate, the crew called for volunteers to grab its edges and hold what was swiftly becoming a balloon down so that it would not take off before its time.

My eldest brother, Peter, volunteered to help; and I watched, horrified, in dread lest the monster break loose and fly away with Peter clutching its hem, screaming as he sailed to the sky, doomed to lose his grip at last and fall into Lake Michigan from outer space. At the last moment, however, someone yelled, "Let it go," and everyone, including Peter, did let go. The great black ball took off with the daredevil balloonist sitting on a narrow board dangling below it, parachute on his back, waving gallantly to us as if he were saying goodbye to earth forever.

We kept our naked eyes fixed on him as he sailed up over the water of the big lake until he was almost out of sight; we shaded our eyes and blinked in mute fascination until someone shouted, "There he goes," and then we all saw his parachute open and watched him float like a Pentecostal dove into the water below, where a motorboat was at hand to fish him out.

Along about five o'clock we would pack up and catch a trolley, this time for Mona Lake, a small dirty lake where people went—not to swim, but to revel in its amusement park. There we would finish off the sandwiches, eat our second banana, and then cluster around my mother to walk with her around the park to see the sights. We looked up into a dark sky where people waved down from their swinging gondolas at the top of the Ferris wheel's awesome circuit, and we waved back to them. We had no money for such thrills ourselves, but, oh, the sight of them was wonder enough.

But the grand spectacle of the whole Fourth was the fireworks. The second coming of Christ should be heralded by so glorious a lighting up of the heavens as we saw above Mona Lake. We stayed deep into the night to behold it all, bedazzled, until the last fantastic explosion of a million colored stars. Then we packed ourselves into another jammed trolley, which took us back to the terminal point at Marquette and Getty; we trudged tired at my mother's side down and up the hill on the two-mile hike home, feeling for sure that we had for one day been given a whopping chunk of life's goodness.

Next day, early, my mother went back to scrubbing the floors of strangers. But for that splendid day she was our assurance that God was on our side. I practice this memory, along with some other good ones, every now and then. It brings me back to where I came from, tells me who I am and what I am for, and gives me a feeling that my life has a footing and may yet be manageable.

As we get some skill in remembering, our memories will grow; we will add memory to memory, and as they increase they will also get richer. They will give us a sense of setting, of where we come from, of time and place and people, all together telling us who we are.

Some of us have to practice redemptive remembering. Our setting was too grim, the people too unloving for persistent sharing, and they can be remembered only in pain. Such memories must be redeemed. We redeem our bad memories by remembering how we found power to survive, how we came through and wrote our story in spite of the rotten setting we had to begin it in.

The Practice of Letting Go

God can forgive wholesale. We need to do it retail. We forgive in increments; it is more like reinvesting small dividends each month than hitting it big in a day.

A few years ago I was enraged by a local police officer who had—I thought—treated someone I love with outrageous brutality. I hated the man; I wanted bad things to happen to him, anything short of being shot in the line of duty. I lost control of a precious part of my own life to my bitterness.

I knew that I would not get my own life back until I forgave him. So I began the slow journey to my own healing.

That was four years ago. Every now and then I have seen this officer driving by in his patrol car. And each time I see him, I need to forgive him all over again. But it gets easier as I keep up the practice.

At no time do we need practice more than when we forgive ourselves. Never am I less in control of myself than when I am dominated by my own self-condemnation. It takes enormous courage to forgive one's own self. And it takes practice.

I recommend that we practice an act of self-forgiveness every day. Here is one way to do it. First, be concrete; recall a single specific thing you did that you know was unworthy. Second, pronounce absolution to yourself; say it out loud: "In the name of God, I forgive you." Third, standing in front of a mirror, look at yourself eyeball to eyeball and repeat at least five times that the God of free grace gives you freedom to forgive yourself. Keep in practice, and you may take the most important step you can take to getting your life under control again.

The Practice of Surrender

In the discipline of surrender we admit to ourselves that we try to get control of our own lives by controlling other people's opinions of us. And then we move on to the practice of surrender. We repeat over and over again to ourselves, alone and aloud, that God's love and our own integrity give us freedom to live without other people's approval. The very repetition of the words becomes a means of grace that brings them alive.

I confess to you that I would rather do almost anything than "gratuitous exercises" of the spirit. They feel artificial to me. But I know that when I refuse to practice, I end up losing control just when I need most to be in control. When I do practice, I am ahead of the game.

❧ ❧

Somewhere, there are some smart people huddled in a high-level staff session, devising ways to take control of our lives. They seduce us, they trick us, and they lie to us; they promise us anything if we will turn control over to them, control of what we buy, how we live, what we will live for, how we will vote, and how we will feel about what matters most. They are out to get control.

And some of us are sitting ducks. We are so tired of the struggle; we don't have the energy for genuine *intentions*. We want to float for a while, like a twig on the Colorado River. Life has become one severe stress after another, and we cannot cope with it, let alone control it. So we swallow the pills. We down the booze. Or we do what other people tell us to do. It's so much easier that way.

The only way back is to take control of our selves. Self-control is story-control, life-control. It is not just about being moderate, levelheaded, cool people who always walk a straight line right down the middle between extremes of passivity and passion. It is about this fundamental issue of our lives: Are we going to determine the direction of our lives? Are we going to write our own stories?

God knows, it's a tough nut. Life is a tough nut. We are not always winners. But we are on the way, which is a pretty good way to be.

CHAPTER 5

An Eye for What Is Really Going On

In January Doris and I were driving north on U.S. 101, heading into Santa Cruz, California, on a Friday afternoon at four o'clock, just as the traffic began to close in. We noticed that the Volkswagen van just ahead of us in the right lane was drifting, and we watched as its front wheel slid off the concrete onto the gravel shoulder. The driver jerked his van back into the lane, but too hard, and he lost control. Helpless against his own momentum, he swung an arc across all four lanes of the northbound freeway.

"Oh, God, he's going to get killed!"

A phalanx of cars barreled down on him. Drivers grabbed their wheels, slammed on their brakes, and swerved out of his way. Somehow the van beached itself on the other side of the four-lane freeway, untouched, upright, stopped by a pile of dirt left behind by a highway maintenance crew. I maneuvered into the left lane, parked on the shoulder, got out, and walked back. The driver, a pudgy fortyish man in blue shirt and jeans, had gotten out and was leaning on the front door of his van. A small child, about eight, was sitting still inside, quiet, perhaps wondering what was happening with her father.

"You okay?"

"Yeah, I'm all right, a little shook up."

"Sure you'll be all right?"

"Yeah, I'll be all right in a few minutes."

"You could have gotten killed."

"Yeah, I lost control"

"Sure you're okay?"

"Yeah, I'll be fine."

I walked back to Doris, told her he was all right, got myself back into our Toyota, and drove off toward Santa Cruz only a few minutes behind schedule.

After ten minutes I began second-guessing myself.

"I should have stayed with the man a while."

"Why? There was nothing you could have done."

"He said he was okay, but he couldn't have been okay. Not after what he had just gone through. I should have seen that."

"Well, it's too late to turn around now. Better forget it."

A few months later, in April, I was being driven down Interstate 91, a four-lane Connecticut expressway, heading into Hartford. It was a few minutes after four, the commuter traffic getting thick but still rolling along. Right ahead of us, in the second lane from the left, the driver of a pickup truck made a sudden lurch to the right to avoid a muffler that had fallen off somebody's car. He missed the muffler, but he swerved hard into the path of a red Ford Escort coming up a length behind and to the right of him.

The driver of the Escort made a frantic twist to the right, got across the right lane, landed her front wheel on the shoulder, then yanked too hard on the steering wheel to get back on the concrete. She hooked it to the left and shot her light compact straight across three lanes.

Straddling the far-left lane, her car swung crazily around in a complete circle, slammed dead still for a second, and then lurched back across the expressway a second time. It settled on the gravel alongside the right lane and stopped, untouched. She should have been crushed. But there she was, sitting on the skirt of the road, on all four wheels, undented, alive.

My companion maneuvered her car to the side. I got out and walked back to the Escort, took a quick look through the windshield, and saw a youngish woman, by herself, holding on to the steering wheel. I opened the door on the passenger side and sat down next to her. She was ashen, her eyes were unfocused, her fingers clamped to the wheel, her body rigid.

I put my hand on hers, and then I took her in my arms, slowly tightened my hold on her, and held her close to me until I felt her body relax a little and heard her whimper some muffled thanks against my chest. I could not think of anything appropriate to say to her, so I prayed, "Oh Lord, you must love this woman much. You must love her very much." I said it over and over again.

CATCHING THE MOMENT OF GRACE

I don't suppose I will ever again see two highway miracles like the ones I saw that year. I replay them in my head every now and then when I am driving the freeways. And two thoughts that come to me are crucial to everything else I need to say in this chapter.

First of all, it strikes me that both of these unusual highway situations were parables of the moments of grace that life gives to us all the time. I met two people on the highway and each of them asked me a simple question: "Now that you are here, and I am here, what are you going to do about me?" They did not put it into words; they asked it by being there, thrown in my path, being where I also happened to be. Each of them offered me a moment of grace to do something creative.

I answered both people in different ways because I saw different things about them. I did not give a helpful answer the first time because I was in a hurry. I did not take the time to see what was probably going on in the mind and body of a man who so narrowly escaped tragedy on U.S. 101. I made a better response the second time because I was primed, in the moment given me, to look deeper into what was probably going on with the young woman who had come so close to getting killed on Interstate 91. In short, the critical difference was how I discerned the situation.

My second thought is that what I did with the young woman in the Escort was certainly not the only thing I could have done. Somebody else might have come along and acted very differently than I did, and done something at least as effective. The moments of grace usually give us more than one good thing we can do, and we do well if we manage a pretty good batting average.

What I did was awfully risky. Most of the time, it would be quite wooden-headed for a tall gray-haired male to open a car door uninvited, plunk himself next to a young women who has never seen him before, and take her in his arms. I might have scared her out of her wits and sent her into an even deeper shock than she was already in. She might have screamed and gotten me into a lot of trouble. It was a gamble.

And yet I did a pretty good thing—a better thing, it seems to me—than I did when I met the driver of the van and left him alone.

My highway stories are small potatoes, to be sure; but they illustrate the difference that a little discernment can make when it comes to growing a good life out of the moments of grace that come our way almost every day. The moment of grace comes to us in the dynamics of any situation we walk into. It is an opportunity that God sews into the fabric of a routine situation. It is a chance to do something creative, something helpful, something healing, something that makes one unmarked spot in the world better off for our having been there. We catch it if we are people of discernment.

All around us, at any hour, people show up who ask us to do something about them. In the kitchen, in the bedroom, in the shop, in the neighborhood, in the oval office, at a party, in a conversation, in a crisis, in a lull, at home, at work, in church, in politics—anywhere, everywhere, somebody may at any moment cross our path and ask us: What are you going to do about me? When they ask it, they give us a moment of grace.

We can write beautiful life stories out of our moments of grace.

Some people think that we make a good life by remembering the ancient moral principles that come to us from the past; when we have to make critical decisions, we simply hew to our principles. Other people think that we make a good life by dreaming dreams for the future; we set our sails and make all our decisions en route by asking which move will take us to where we want to go. There is something to be said for both points of view.

But there is another way of making a good life. The American scholar H. Richard Niebuhr suggested that we look at life as a conversation: as we enter each new situation, we engage in a conversation with it. It asks us a question. We listen. We make our response. And then we go on to another situation. Gradually we create our lives by the responses we give to the people we meet in all the different situations where we meet them.

The important point for this chapter is that we usually make good answers if we hear the question well. But since the questions are not usually put into words, we have to listen with our eyes and our feelings and our hearts. In other words, to create a good life we need to be people of discernment. We need an eye for the subtle shadings and loose stitches in the fabric of our relationships with people.

What I am calling discernment, the ancient Greeks called *practical wisdom,* or *prudence,* and said it was the main hinge on which the gates of human excellence turn. It is, in philosopher Josef Pieper's words, the "mother and mold of all virtue." A wise person has an eye for what is really going on, and then has a practical sense for the better thing to do about it. The book of Proverbs puts it this way: "Wisdom reposes in the heart of the discerning" (14:33).

We discern things on two levels. One is the cognitive level of perception; here we simply see what is going on within any human situation. The other is the level of imagination; here we see more deeply and also get an insight into the sort of response that might be creative and helpful. There are no standardized labels for these two levels; I'm going to settle for *cognitive* discernment and *imaginative* discernment.

WHAT THE DISCERNING PERSON SEES

I am going to be talking here about *cognitive* discernment. About the things that any discerning person sees and duller people miss.

A discerning person notices details. She sees the fine details that can make huge differences, like a slight shift in someone's tone of voice, a gesture, a falling of the eyes, a shift of emphasis, a change of color. She knows that the world sometimes turns on molehills and that tempests blow in teacups.

A discerning person notices the differences between things. He sees the difference, for instance, between what is real and what is just talk, between what is important and what is trivial, between what needs action now and what can wait until the next day. He sees the fine-drawn shadings that set a minor but genuine work of art off from a smashing poster. And if he is a discerning doctor he can tell the difference between treating the symptoms of cancer and treating the complex human being who suffers them.

A discerning person sees the connections between things. She notices the links between what happened last week and what is happening today. She sees that someone's odd behavior today is somehow connected to a nasty thing someone said to her last week. She observes that someone's symptoms are suspiciously like the symptoms she saw in another patient a year ago, alike enough to suspect a common cause. A moment of grace is often lurking in the connections we see between two different situations.

A discerning person sees things going on beneath the surface. He sees hints of how a person is really feeling behind the facade of his smile. He feels the pain his friend is smothering beneath a snide remark she makes. He senses the undercurrents of hurt beneath his secretary's curt readiness to run an errand for him.

A discerning person knows a book is worth reading even if it is not a bestseller. She can tell you what a subtle movie is really all about without reading the reviews. And she can tell when a bargain is really a bargain, because she recognizes quality when she sees it. A discerning person has the makings of a connoisseur.

THE BASIC SKILLS

Discernment is not simply a trait some of us inherit from our parents. Getting to be a person of discernment is a lot like learning how to play golf. A man who can fix his eyes on a small white ball and can keep his arms stiff while he swings a club has the natural gifts to become a pretty good golfer. But he will become a golfer only if he is willing to develop some skills.

In the same way, if we can keep our eyes and ears open to what is happening in and around us, we have the makings of a person of discernment. But to develop a keen sense for the realities inside all the voices buzzing around us, we have to develop our natural skills. So I want to review some of the skills we need.

It Takes Awareness

After a career of watching people succeed and fail, psychologist Erich Fromm concluded that many people fail simply because they do not see what is happening around them or in them. And they do not see it because they are half-asleep. "The paradoxical situation with a vast number of people today," he wrote in *The*

Art of Loving, "is that they are half asleep when awake, and half awake when asleep." They do not wake up and see when they stand at a fork in the road and have to decide; they miss the moment of grace because they are not paying attention.

A person has to be awake to see where an innocent flirtation at five o'clock in the afternoon is almost certain to end by midnight. We have to be awake to notice that a charming persuader is manipulating us for his own ends. We have to be awake at dinner to sense that our companion has a burden that she wants us to notice without her having to say it. We have to be awake to what is happening inside of ourselves, too, while we struggle to survive and maybe succeed in a corporation that does not care if we compromise our conscience as long as we hang tough with the competition.

The discerning person has to be awake to what is going on, the way a fastball pitcher needs to watch what a runner on first base is up to while he is also concentrating on the batter.

It Takes an Honest Memory

We always see what is happening today through our memory of what happened yesterday. And we miss the critical reality of the *now* if we do not keep an honest memory of the *then*.

Fred Dickson decided to stop drinking three weeks ago. For years he had joined three colleagues at Monahan's for a few Chivas Regals after work on Friday to celebrate survival of the week past and to hail the blessed advent of the weekend coming. Last Friday, just two weeks since his decision to quit, his friends saw him outside the office at noon and reminded him that they were meeting for the usual at five.

He told himself that he deserved a little partying after a long week, and he did not want to be the one to break up the old gang. He also told himself that he did not need a drink to enjoy the party. So he went along.

He forgot that those preweekender celebrations had a liturgy that needed alcohol the way a baptism needs water. Everything he enjoyed about the Friday fellowship was coiled around a liquor glass the way Thanksgiving Day is centered on a dining room table. First, the comfort of the bartender's cordial, "Good evening gentlemen, the usual?" (Oh the pride of being known by what you drink in a classy Manhattan bar!) Then the in-house gossip, a couple of boorish jokes about the new secretary in the boss's office, the first sip and its ensuing sigh of gratification, another round of the same, and then a limpid descent into the banal consolations of alcoholic *gemütlichkeit.*

Before they stopped laughing at the office joke, it became as inevitable as the coming of Saturday that Fred was going to say, "Oh well, after all, I deserve one," and that he would end up slightly south of sobriety, sluggishly shuffling to the subway, hooked again.

People like Fred do not have bad memories. They are not honest with their good memories. And they lose discernment when they need it most.

It Takes Control

To see the little things that make a difference, we need to keep our cool. Hot feelings can bring on a temporary case of blindness.

Anger, one of nature's most creative passions, can blind us when it flies out of control. People who fly off the handle lose sight of reality until they land on earth again. Sexual passion, one of God's best inventions, can render the best of us deaf, dumb, and blind to what is really happening to us in some seductive moment when all our hormonal systems say go. A tremor of desire touched off when sensuous skin touches sensuous skin can shake our senses and cause a temporary blindness to what is really going on. This is the bewitchery of passion: Life is flat and boring without it, but passion can jam the voice of reality.

It Takes a Willingness to Listen

To listen is to wait in silence for the revelation of a mystery. There is a mystery waiting to be revealed in all the voices that speak to us, the quiet voices, the loud voices, the angry voices, the friendly voices, the seductive voices, the ugly voices, the hateful voices, and the loving voices. There is always something being said inside of what is being said. Standing still amid the voices that flow from the realities that touch our lives, waiting to hear what is there to be heard, to be heard in and under and over all the shouting and all the whispering—this is listening.

Dr. Richard Linger, a distinguished internist now retired, admitted once that every time he misdiagnosed a patient he was too busy to pay attention to the whole story the patient was telling him. His patients would begin to tell him their symptoms. He would catch the first couple of complaints and then stop listening, noting that the first two symptoms were familiar signs of a familiar disease. He would decide on his diagnosis then and there, without listening for more. He sometimes misdiagnosed his patient's condition because he stopped listening too soon. Bad medicine, sometimes fatal medicine, followed. Sometimes we have to hear before we can see.

It Takes Focus

Nobody can take in everything. Unless we are God, which none of us is, or a genius, which few of us are, we need to discriminate.

The first time Doris and I visited Rome, we hoofed it around the ancient city, trying to take in everything worth looking at. We feasted on antiquities and local color; and by two o'clock in the afternoon, when we finally made it into a fine museum we had come to Rome to see, we no longer saw what our eyes were looking at.

Most of us overdose on data these days. We are bombarded with information. There is a computer that operates at a trillionth of a second and can get the data on almost anything for us so fast that we cannot even measure the speed. Even hearing that such a computer exists only increases our sense of information glut.

We are not only dizzied by real, but unimportant, facts, we are overstimulated by illusions of reality. Images created by the media out of what is not even going on. Our minds, already boggled by reality, are clobbered by unreality, nonevents created to look like events. Men and women are paid enormous sums of money to feed us on the fantasy that we are seeing something real when we are only seeing fakery. They hook us with lively pictures and, if we stay hooked, we lose our own power to discern what is really real.

To escape from this deluge of things that don't matter and things that did not even happen, some of us drink alcohol or take drugs or watch television, or all three, which lowers our powers of discernment to the lowest notch.

Henk Pander is different. He is an artist, a good one, a cousin of mine. He is intentionally blind to ninety percent of the fuss and frets of his environment. He never watches television news. He has nothing to do with computers. He does not notice that his roof needs fixing, his lawn needs mowing, his car needs washing, or his shirts need ironing. But, oh, the things he does see in the realities that he does choose to look at!

So one way to develop discernment is to limit our factual intake. There are millions of things that clamor for our attention that we are no worse off for not knowing. Millions of things we should pay no attention to whatsoever. But it is up to us to turn our eyes away from them, the way we turn off a television set. We do not need to know everything. We need to focus on what matters most.

For Some People It Comes by Intuition

Carl Jung said that a person with intuition "has a keen nose for things in the bud." William Manchester says that Winston Churchill had a zigzag streak of lightning in his brain, the intuition that pierced straight through all the helter-skelter of detail into its sometimes terrifying significance.

Once the exiled Russian writer, Aleksandr Solzhenitsyn, had gotten the hang of life in Stalin's prisons, it did not take him long to learn that they were full of spies dressed in the rags of prisoners. The spies would pry secrets out of the poor dupes who trusted them, and then betray them; any prisoner who was thus gulled was done for. But Solzhenitsyn was never fooled. Not once during his terrible time in the Gulag Archipelago did he get taken in.

He saw through every spy he met. And the amazing

thing is that he did not know *how* he knew. He could not detect any signals that gave them away. By some instant, subrational intuition, he knew who was a spy and who was not a spy.

I have been with my daughter Cathy in the presence of someone neither of us had known before and after ten minutes she would walk away saying, "He's a phony." And I have chided her for jumping to conclusions only to have events prove that her immediate intuition was absolutely right. I have virtually no intuition; I could be swindled by any amateur confidence man who put on a sincere mask. Jesus had powers of intuition that were intensified beyond anything human; he saw intuitively the pure heart inside of a sinner and the stale pride behind the whitewashed fence of the Pharisee.

It is a dangerous route to knowledge, this zigzag streak of lightning. A person who intuits things correctly one day can be completely misled the next. Intuitive people need some ordinary straight-lined observers around them for constant reality checks. But even if we cannot trust it all the way, we are fools to ignore the gift of this intuitive shaft of light that pierces the crust into the core of reality.

These, then, are some of the skills we need to develop if we are going to become people of discernment. We don't need all of them in equal amounts. Some of us will major in a few; others will develop several.

Most of us were born with healthy, vital, inquisitive, alert minds. And some of us have the gift of intuition besides. But these are only the raw materials. If we have them, we still need to practice them the way a great pianist like Arthur Rubinstein, at the very top of his genius, still kept his fingers in form by everlastingly running through the same scales any fretful child has to bang away at when she first begins to play.

Discerning people are made, not born; and all of us have a chance to develop the skill of discernment. But the skills we have been talking about so far, though utterly unexpendable, are not enough. We need imaginative discernment to catch the moment of grace.

With cognitive discernment we could become shrewd operators—cunning, crafty, and clever. We could be astute observers of events and connoisseurs of fine things. We could catch weaknesses in a person's defenses and seduce him to buy when he should put his money in a certificate of deposit. But we would miss the moment of grace that any moment may offer us to move beyond cunning and competence into a graceful style of life.

We need one more thing with which to catch the moment of grace.

BY LOVE'S CLEAR LIGHT

Let us say that we have the facts of the matter. Let us also say that we have enough discernment to sense what is *really* going on. We are alert; we have an honest memory; we keep cool while others get hysterical; we listen; we keep things in focus; and maybe we even have some intuition. What more do we need to recognize the moment of grace when it comes?

What we need is imagination. We need imagination to see the reality of people beneath the cluster of annoying circumstances. We need imagination to see through the labels we put on people. We need imagination to catch the elusive instant that offers us, every now and then, a new chance to make creative responses to the challenges of life. The question is, how do we get the imagination?

There is one power that gives us the imagination to recognize the moment of grace when it comes. It is the power of love. Of caring love, mind you; of the sort of love that can put our most legitimate desires on the back burner in order to care for another person's needs. This is love with imagination. Erotic love stimulates fantasies, and fantasies can distort what we see. But caring love can open our eyes to things erotic love does not see.

Let me explain why I believe this is so. Eighty percent of what we see in front of us lies behind our eyes. We filter what we see through our fears of things that might happen and through our memories of things that have happened. We filter them through our dogmas of how things ought to be and through our feelings about how they are. Thus we look at what is going on through lenses ground by our hopes and our fears.

This is where love can do its work. It gives us the ability to see through reality as we want it into reality as it is. This is surely why the apostle Paul made so much of the combination of love and discernment: "It is my prayer," he said in his letter to the Philippians, "that your love may abound more and more, with knowledge and all discernment, so that you may approve what is excellent" (1:9,10, RSV).

So the equation is: Love added to cognitive discernment gives us imaginative discernment. And this provides the depth perception we need for excellence the way a doctor with bold imagination added to his normal skills stands out as an artist in a field of competent surgeons.

Let us look at some tricks that love has up its sleeve to give us imaginative discernment.

Love Gets Us Involved

Experts used to tell us that if we expect to see things right, we have to be detached from what we are looking at. Objectivity! Staying aloof, and drawing inferences by strictly monitored scientific methods—this was the route to knowing.

In the middle of this century a philosopher named Michael Polanyi came along. In his book *Personal Knowledge* he taught us to take a deeper look at how we get to know things. There are some things we get to know only by getting personally involved with them—only by being part of them, caring about them, having a deep feeling of attachment with them. In short, according to Polanyi, we can know some things only by loving them.

Take one of America's finer novelists, John Steinbeck, who wrote so powerfully about poor, humble people who lived in the West during the hard years. His masterpiece *The Grapes of Wrath* was a story about the people who were blown away from their Oklahoma farms by the terrible dust storms of the 1930s. Steinbeck saw what was really going on in the lives of those desperate people as they made their hungry journey across the mean desert in their broken-down jalopies on their way to a new and fertile land they believed was waiting for them in golden California.

Steinbeck ate and slept with them in the cold mud and raw filth of the migrant camps. He cared about their pains, cared about their hungers, their anger, their fear, their failures, their meanness, their tenderness; and he shared their troubles. His love gave him eyes to see the immense nobility of Ma Joad doing everything she had to do to keep her family together. Love gave him eyes to see the fragile miracle of frail Rose of Sharon who, having lost her newborn baby, gave suck to an old, old man dying of hunger. Even today, if you read *The Grapes of Wrath* you know that Steinbeck's love for the Okies gave him the imagination to see the nobility they kept alive inside of themselves in their struggle to survive.

Or take an impressionist artist like Monet. Surely

he could see the beauty of the landscapes he painted so lushly only because he loved the country so much. And he could put the lavish beauty of it on canvas because he even loved the oils and brushes he painted it with. Michelangelo saw exquisite things in the human form because he loved human beings, but he also loved his chisel and the marble he worked with. Artists see what is going on because they are involved in a love affair with reality.

Getting involved does wonders for our eyes. A few years before the Civil Rights movement had begun, when I was a young minister in Paterson, New Jersey, some parents threatened to leave the church the day that we accepted black people into our fellowship. I knew I could not argue them out of their fears. So I persuaded the women to work with us in our vacation Bible school, knowing that they would have black children in their classes. They agreed. Two weeks of involvement with these beautiful children opened my parishioners' eyes to the wonderful, responsive, spiritual human beings the black children were.

Love Sees Through Our Labels

We put our labels on people the way designers sew labels on their clothes. And then we let the labels tell us who people are and what they are worth. If we value intelligence in children, we label them as fast learners or slow learners, and the first question we ask about any child is how he or she is doing at school. If we value money, we label people as well-to-do or poor, and the first thing we wonder about people is how much money they make. If we value physical appearance, we label people as attractive or unattractive, and the first thing we ask about a person is what he or she looks like.

Here is a church group that puts a premium on stable families and lasting marriages: When a woman in that church gets a divorce, the church labels her a divorced woman, and blinds itself to her reality, to her pains, to her gifts, to her needs. I am also familiar with a group that is offended by homosexuality: When a man comes along who is homosexual, the group labels him gay, and blinds itself to the complex, gifted, sensitive person he is. We belong to a society that values physical power: When people come along who are physically disabled, we label them disabled, and we thereby blind ourselves to the infinite treasure they have to offer us.

We never caricature people with our labels more decisively than when they hurt us unfairly. When someone I trusted lets me down and does me wrong, I immediately label that person in my memory as the clod who hurt me. The only reality he has for me is what I have printed on my label. He really is a weak, needy, and flawed person, complex and convoluted, who probably tried to compensate for his own weakness by hurting me.

Love gives us the imagination to see a divorced

man or woman as a complex person; the homosexual man or woman as a whole person; and the man or woman with disabilities as a beautifully gifted person. Even the person who unfairly wounded us becomes a person bigger than the wound he or she caused. And when we discern the deeper reality, we are in a position to respond more creatively when such people as these walk into our lives and ask, "Now that I am here with you, what will you do about me?"

Love Sees Through Our Insecurities

I have often walked into ordinary social circles so insecure about myself that all I could see in them was the opportunity they offered me to fall on my face. As I entered their circle my mind was fixed on myself and how I would come across. Would these people like me? Would they even notice me? Would they think my ideas are worth hearing? Or would they think I am slightly ridiculous? As long as I kept thinking about how I was coming across to them, I could not see what was going on with them. I missed the moment of grace they offered me.

There are two ways that love helps me to see real people through the filter of my insecurities.

One of them is a growing power to love myself enough to be thankful for what I am, and to forgive myself for what I am not. I feel this power intermittently, I admit, but I feel it often enough to get my eyes off my anxieties about myself and get a focus on what is going on with other people.

Love also helps me to get outside of myself long enough to discover that the people whose favor I need so much are as weak and needy as I am. They are trusting me to care about them while I am struggling to see them through the haze of my own anxieties. If I discern them in their needs, I am getting the imagination to catch a moment of grace when it comes.

Love Sees Beyond the Winner's Circle

A few years ago I spent a hot August day at the Los Angeles county jail, waiting for the wheels of the system to open jail doors for someone I was bailing out. It takes a long time to spring somebody out of this mammoth prison, so I had to wait and watch.

I watched the pimps in white suits bailing out their whores; lawyers in black suits bailing out their clients; drug dealers bailing out their peddlers; girls bailing out their boyfriends; and drunks who disturbed the peace the night before slinking out on their own. As I took in the sleazy parade, I began to see everyone in it as a full-time, obsessive-compulsive, addictive, hopeless loser. By noon I lost any desire to know anything more about them than that.

At midafternoon I decided to go out for a cold drink. As I walked out the door I met a lanky black man wearing a black suit with a priest's collar—a prison chaplain, I figured, on his way out at the end of a day's work of grace. I introduced myself on our way to the parking lot. He gave me the feeling that he had time to talk awhile, so I asked him to join me for a drink.

"Glad to," he said, "there's a Denny's right around the block."

It turned out he wasn't a priest; he was an insurance salesman. He devoted one day out of every week to bring a moment of grace to men locked up in the county jail. He wore the cloth so that everyone there knew what he was up to.

I asked him the sorts of questions any decent Pharisee would ask.

"Don't you keep meeting the same people, coming in and going out? Recidivists, repeaters, losers?"

"Well," he replied, "every person locked up in that jail has got somebody with a key to let him out. But I meet people in my business every day who are locked up in a cell inside their hearts and nobody on earth has a key to let them out. So I don't see an enormous difference between them."

"Okay, true enough, but still, aren't most of the men you meet inside *this* jail hard-core losers?"

"Well, maybe they are, but that's just not the way I divide people up. The only two categories of people I really care about are the forgiven people and the unforgiven people."

He had me.

"I met Jesus today," I told Doris when I came home.

"Oh yeah? What did he say to you?"

"He told me I was a Pharisee. Have eyes. Don't see."

The Pharisees were good people, but some of them were good only in a shallow, legalistic sort of way. For them life was a serious game. The object was to score points with God. Score enough points and you win. Score too few and you lose. So the Pharisees divided all the people they knew into two groups: winners and losers in the game of getting on with God. When Jesus met them he said, "You have eyes to see, but you see nothing. You have ears to hear, but you hear nothing." My friend, the minister-insurance salesman, had eyes to see, and he saw things that I, on that hot August day, could not see.

Love Sees Through Our Rights

I have the eyes of an eagle for other people's rights—as long as they do not interfere with my rights. But let anybody stake a claim to what I think is mine by right, and I suddenly have the discernment of a groundhog. Anyone who gets in the way of my rights is therewith transformed before my eyes into a scoundrel or a blockhead.

When I was eighteen years old, fresh out of Muskegon Senior High, I went to work doing the dirtiest chores on the grounds of a little shop called Smedes Iron Works, which my uncle operated in his back yard on the east side of Detroit. I mostly dipped angle irons—the irons that support large windowsills in a brick building—into a tank of gaseous black pitch that filled the windowless room with dizzying fumes.

I have never had a job I hated as much as I hated dipping angle irons into that black tank and stacking them up one by one in crisscross rows to dry. So, mostly to get my mind off iron for a couple of nights a week, I rode the Mack Avenue trolley into downtown Detroit, where I was enrolled in some evening classes at Cass Tech High School.

I took typing, just in case I ever got enough confidence to go to college. And, with the hunch that I might one day improve my lot in life if I learned how to talk, I also enrolled in a class in public speaking. It was in the public speaking class that I met Barney Golden.

Barney was a labor organizer for Walter Reuther's new labor union, the United Auto Workers (UAW), at the Ford Motor Company. He took a shine to me, noticed I had a certain gift of gab, told me I had a future in the labor movement, and offered me a job. I chose to go to school instead.

Barney, however, did get me interested in Henry Ford. I learned, for instance, what Ford really believed in. Ford believed in his rights. He believed that the only person connected with the auto industry who had any rights inside a shop was the man whose name was on the building.

Workers had no rights at all. They had no right to make a contribution to how the shop was run. No right to know the boss's plans for the company. They did not even have a right to share their own private thoughts with someone in the sanctum of the bathroom. And they certainly had no right to organize a labor union to speak for them. Once a man set his foot inside Henry Ford's shop, he was reduced from a person to a hand, a hired hand at that; and as far as Henry Ford was concerned, hands did not have rights.

When Henry Ford discovered that working men and women were laying claim to some rights of their own, they became his enemies. And a union organizer who got a hired hand to thinking about his rights was the devil himself. The only way to deal with union men was to destroy them. So Ford hired a Navy prizefighter by the name of Harry Bennett to beat down anyone who flirted with the union. Bennett in turn organized a squadron of thugs who slugged the union organizers bloody with iron bars.

Henry Ford could see through any piston engine, but when it came to the people who made the engines, he could not see beyond their slot alongside the assembly line.

Max De Pree is another sort of industrial leader. He is chairman emeritus and former CEO of the furniture company, Herman Miller, Inc. De Pree certainly knew that he had certain rights when it came to running the company. And, as far as I can tell, he was not inclined to give up a single one of them.

What made Max De Pree different from Henry Ford was his ability to see through his own rights into the rights of real people around him. He saw that every employee was a unique person, a complex person: maybe a poet as well as a millwright, a soul aspiring to eternity as well as a stock clerk aspiring to better wages. And he could see that once such a person set foot in the shop, he or she was a partner in an enterprise of living importance to them both.

As De Pree sees it, we develop the art of leading people only if we see them whole, as people who have rights of their own within the corporation. He wrote a book about running a corporation called *Leadership Is an Art*. He begins his theory of business leadership first by conceding the rights of the people who work in his shop, and then committing himself to honor their rights.

He sees every worker as a person endowed with a right to be recognized, not as a hired hand, but as a person the company needs as much as that person needs the company. He also sees the worker as a person with the right to be involved in determining how the company is run. Every worker has a right to a personal covenant in which a boss and a subordinate are equally committed to each other's success. He sees the worker as a person with a right to know the company's problems and goals; and, finally, he sees that every worker has a right to share in the company's ownership and in the company's risks.

Henry Ford would have thought that Max De Pree had lost his mind. In fact, while Henry Ford led his own company to the edge of self-destruction, Herman

Miller, Inc. has become a very profitable manufacturer of superbly styled office furniture. And it is on Fortune's list of the one hundred best companies in America to work for.

One particular incident gives us a clue to the source of De Pree's imagination.

As CEO De Pree met with his managers each month. He naturally chaired the meeting. At one of the meetings De Pree read a letter from the mother of a handicapped employee. She had written to thank the people at Herman Miller for their efforts to make life more meaningful for people who are disadvantaged. Halfway through the letter the CEO broke down and wept in front of the senior managers of the corporation. One of the senior vice presidents walked up the center aisle, put his arm around his boss, kissed him on the cheek, and adjourned the meeting.

If Henry Ford ever shed a tear for a Ford worker, it went unobserved and unrecorded.

Love Sees Through Our Good Intentions

In my book *Choices* I recalled an episode in my life that revealed how my own good intentions could blind me to what was really going on in the very human being for whom I intended good. I was visiting friends in Nairobi, the capital of Kenya, and they invited me to travel up into the country to the little village where my friend's mother still lived. Driving with us was a young woman who had come down from the village to work as a domestic in Nairobi. But the big city was a terror to her and she had to go home again.

A couple of hours out of Nairobi, we spotted a small hotel left from the days when Kenya was a British colony. We were hungry because we had left Nairobi without having had lunch, so we stopped. The four of us went into the oak-ribbed Victorian dining room: my married friends—one of them white and the other black—the young Kenyan, and myself.

We were served with a stuffy gracefulness by a team of waiters in black tie. First a cold drink. The young villager did not touch hers. Then a lukewarm bowl of soup. She did not lift her hands off her lap. By this time we began to see what was going on. A frightened person was suffering because we did not have enough imagination to sense what being a guest in that elegant hotel would do to her. Already dislocated by the frenzy of the city, now she was hauled into a plush palace that displaced her completely.

We were offered a moment of grace, but we could not see it because we were blinded by our good intentions. With a little imagination we might have ordered some sandwiches that we could have eaten along the road with no embarrassment to our companion. As it was, we hurt her; not because we had low morals or bad motives, but because we did not have enough imagination. We let our own good intentions block our discernment.

These are just a few ways in which caring love added to cognitive discernment makes for imaginative discernment—a sense for the deeper dimensions in what is going on, a feel for the moment of grace that invites us to give a helpful answer to the question somebody is asking us.

TESTING OUR DISCERNMENT

If we have the power to love, we have an edge, a real edge; but we do not have a guarantee that we will see things as they really are. Or that the response we give is a very helpful and appropriate answer to the question. Did we really catch the moment of grace? Who can be sure?

A person of discernment can be wrong sometimes, is hardly ever totally right. And we are all better off when we have enough discernment to know that we could at any moment be quite mistaken, all wrong—or only half-right—about what we think we see.

We are not zapped with imaginative discernment. We get it by working at our native skills and by keeping our hearts open to love. It takes practice, and it never comes with a certainty that no one can contradict.

Love enhances our ability to see what is happening in the lives of people around us, but it does not relieve us of our human limits. When philosopher Josef Pieper said that discernment was the key to all virtue, he had the good sense to warn us not to "expect certainty where it cannot exist."

A good way to test our discernment is to share what we see with people who are looking at the same situation with us. They are seeing it through their own lenses, of course. They are as prone to shortsightedness as we are. They could be wrong. But they could also see something that we have missed. We need what the older philosophers called *docility,* a willingness to listen to people who may be able to correct our vision.

The primary reason people of good will disagree on the vexing and troubling matters of our time is not that some people are smart and others are stupid; nor is it because moral people are on one side and immoral people are on the other. We disagree mostly because we see things differently. And we see things differently because we filter everything we see through a grid of our own fears, pains, bitter or sacred memories, angers, and loves. Even people who love well can see things differently.

Because our discernment is *always*—not sometimes, but always—partial, we need communities of shared discernment. We urgently need communities where we stifle the shouts and listen to each other, listen with the anticipation that every person who speaks to us may have seen something we have missed. In a real community we do not listen to each other the way disciples listen to a guru. Or talk to each other the way the prophet proclaims the word to his followers. We will listen to each other because we have the grace to know that others may see reality just a little more deeply, and a little more truly, than we do.

People with cognitive discernment have a good sense of what is really going on. They see the little things that could make a big difference. They sense what people around them are feeling. They perceive how one thing is related to another, how one thing is different from another, and how one thing is more important than another.

But we need imaginative discernment to catch the moment of grace that offers us an opportunity to do something helpful and constructive. We still need the basic skills. We need to keep awake, keep an honest memory, keep our cool, keep listening, maintain some focus, and respect our own intuition. But to become the sort of people who can be counted on in the moment of grace, we need to let what we see pass through the filter of imaginative love.

CHAPTER 6

A Flair for Loving Fair

Sid and Margie McLief sat tight-lipped and stiff-backed, their legs crossed and their dangling right feet wagging jerky arcs behind a marriage counselor's cluttered desk. The brass-studded leather chairs they were sitting on were pointed at the counselor from opposite corners of the desk so that, with the three of them forming an equilateral triangle, they could talk and yet avoid the strain of looking at each other.

The McLiefs had wed twelve years earlier in a vacant lot behind Sid's apartment house on the north side of Pasadena, California, to the cadence of a life-exalting liturgy that they had composed the night before. At the crest of the service, which devoutly dodged any rumors of God and commitment, the clergyman united the two of them with a hula hoop that he tossed cleanly over their shoulders just before the bridesmaid dumped a basket of wilted gazania blossoms on their heads. And so, having promised to live together as long as love should last, they became man and wife, of sorts.

But their love did not last, and neither did their shared dedication to living an unfettered life. Ten years into their marriage Sid became a stockbroker at

E. F. Hutton, while Margie went on dabbling in abstract tapestries. Their life together was strained. They were just about ready to dissolve their partnership on grounds of a values gap when a friend persuaded them that, as a token of concern for their ten-year-old daughter, they should at least have a talk with a counselor before splitting up. And here they were, misplaced children of the late 1960s, laying their burdens at the feet of a therapist.

It was a rough go that first day of counseling. Margie and Sid had been needling each other with complaints that neither had dared raise above a rumble when they were alone. Margie was ahead on points, but Sid scored with a mean jab at her sloppy lifestyle. She never, *never* performed the fundamentals that, in his reformed view of the world, women were cut from nature's cloth to perform: never got the house cleaned, never ironed his shirts, never put a decent meal on the table on time. She was, when it came down to it, a lazy slob who failed to be a proper woman and a wife unto him.

Margie had neither wit nor will to counterpunch. She could only resort to the aboriginal murmur that soured lovers mutter when lost love turns mean:

"That's not fair."

It *wasn't* fair, the counselor agreed.

But Sid jabbed back, cunningly, he thought:

"I promised to love you. I never said anything about being fair."

THE SORTS OF THINGS LOVERS DO

Love is the heart's power for union with another human being. But, be it weak or strong, love with no fairness in it can make the union hard to bear. As Margie learned, the flat hand of unfair love smarts worse than no love at all.

So we must talk of fairness in love. We will begin by talking of love. Then of fairness. And finally of a love that is fair.

Love flows in two currents. One current flows from our weakness to another's strength. The other current flows from our strength to another's weakness. One is a *seeking* love and the other a *giving* love. Two currents, one love.

The ancient Greeks had eyes mostly for seeking love, the love that drives our restless hearts to seek their rest in whatever looks beautiful and good. They named it *eros*. To love someone erotically is to desire, and need, and therefore to reach out for him or her in a fond hope that this one particular person will satisfy our yearnings. It is the love that seeks a lover, a friend, or God, always out of need.

The early Christians flowed with the opposite current of giving love, the love that moves us in our fullness to give ourselves and our goods to another in need of them. They named it *agape*. Agape is the heart's power to love anyone—lovely or ugly, lovable or repulsive—not because he gives us what we need, but because he needs what we can give.

Both currents alternate inside of a single love. We feel its energy differently one moment to another and with one person or another. Sometimes we feel weak and empty; then our love seeks someone who will fill us and give us strength. Sometimes we feel strong and full; then love enables us to give ourselves to someone weaker and emptier than we are. Lovers are forever trading roles. This time I am weak and you are strong. Tomorrow I will be strong and you will be weak. Two currents, one love.

Whether we love from weakness or from strength, in seeking or giving, our love must be fair or it will blight both our love and our life.

THE SORTS OF THINGS FAIR PEOPLE DON'T DO

Fair people try to be evenhanded, aboveboard, square dealers, measure for measure all the way. When they divvy up whatever they have to share, they try to find a nice balance between what some people deserve and what other people need. Maybe they give more to those who need more. But when they give more to some, they do it not to show favor but to get things a little closer to equal for everyone.

In theory it is not difficult to know what is fair. When it comes to specifics, however, it is easier to recognize fair people by what they do not do than by what they do. As Aristotle said, we know best what is fair at the moment when we have been treated unfairly.

So let's sketch out just a few examples of the sorts of things a fair person does not do.

Fair People Do Not Take Advantage of People in Trouble

During the last year of World War II, people in Amsterdam were starving, while the farmers up north in the flatlands of Friesland had plenty to eat. So hungry city people would stuff a few family treasures into their bags and send the strongest among them up over the Afsluit Dike into Friesland, where a person could still dig something good to eat out of the ground. They would trade their treasures to the Frisian farmers for a few potatoes and, if they struck it right, some cabbage and carrots to take back to their families in Amsterdam.

One woman's negotiable treasure finally came down to her wedding ring. But who can eat a gold ring? She traded it for a pound of potatoes.

The village pastor got a sniff of the foul wind blowing through the village. At service the next Sunday he told the congregation that he knew the name of the farmer who had taken a stranger's wedding ring for a sack of potatoes.

"If the guilty person does not drop the ring in the bag at next Sunday's collection, I shall expose him from this pulpit."

Now these collection bags were velvet sacks dangling between two wooden handles. You could stuff your loose change into them before the person sitting next to you had a chance to notice what you put in. When the deacons emptied the bags the next Sunday, they found fifteen gold wedding rings among the stuivers and the guilders.

Fair People Do Not Refuse to Bear Their Share of the Burden

When Japan went to war with the Western Allies, it already had control of much of mainland China. Japanese authorities rounded up Westerners who lived in China and herded them together in a compound near Shantung. They packed two thousand people into the camp, a haphazard collection of strangers, business-people, missionaries, lawyers, doctors, teachers, senior citizens, children, and a few prostitutes. They had no laws, no leaders, only a forced need to get along.

None of them had a legal right to anything. They could not claim, "I paid for this room." They could not plead a privileged status because of who they were before the internment. And they could not stake out the best spots for themselves on grounds that they inherited them. They had the ultimate equality of those who have nothing.

If these strangers were going to survive together in anything resembling a human community, the thing they needed most was a shared sense for what was fair. For one thing, who would be the leaders? Did it matter that this person was educated or that person was holy or that one had been rich and powerful before the war? And how was the space to be divided? Who were to get the larger rooms? How were the rations to be divided? Was age a consideration? Did children get as much as older people? And who would clean the over-worked, primitive toilets? Nobody could take anything for granted. They had only their sense of fairness to guide them.

Some of the biggest headaches were caused by the smallest things—like how much space one had to lie down on at night. In one small room, eleven men slept on the floor, lying like spoons cradled into each other's curves. They had barely space to turn in their sleep. Across the hall was another room, exactly the same size. But only nine men slept in that room.

The men from the room with eleven men sent two spokesmen to the housing committee. They asked the committee to shift one of their eleven men to the room with nine men. That way both rooms would have the same number of men.

"Surely that's fair enough, isn't it, chaps?"

Langdon Gilkey, who chronicled the whole story in his book *Shantung Compound,* happened to be housing chairman. "I felt elated. Here at last was a per-fectly clear-cut case. Anybody who could count and measure could see the inequity involved."

So he walked over to the room where nine men slept, sure that everyone there would see that taking another man into their room would be the only fair thing to do. But when he got inside the room, he could feel their hostility almost at once. One of them, a British engineer, spoke for the rest of them:

> Sure we're sorry for those chaps over there. But
> what has that got to do with us? We're plenty
> crowded here as it is, and their worries are their
> tough luck. Listen, old boy, we're not crowding up
> for you or for anyone, [and] if you put one of
> them in here, we are merely heaving him out again.

So much for humanity's unspoiled instinct for fair play. We all have twenty-twenty vision for what's fair when we are on the short end. Our vision gets cloudy when we are sitting pretty.

Fair People Do Not Take Advantage of Privileged Information

In Southern California these days, the price of a modest house is killing young peoples' chances of owning a place of their own. But I had a nifty plan for helping my son and his wife buy a small house for themselves. Charlie had just earned his construction license and was now legally qualified to be an independent contractor. So we would buy a ramshackle place that needed a lot of fixing up. I would provide the down payment and he, with his skills, would make it livable.

But every down-at-the-mouth property that looked promising to us looked even more promising to the broker, who made first contact with the person who wanted to sell it. So she scooped it up for herself and then listed it for sale to the public. Total fakery. By the time potential buyers heard of the property, she had probably already hired painters to give it a quick face lift before she sold it next month for forty thousand more than she paid for it. Meanwhile, ordinary suckers traipsed out to the house, made bona fide offers to buy it, and were told that they were just a tad too late.

Fair people know that it isn't fair to make believe they are really acting as honest brokers when, in fact, they are using insiders' information to their own advantage.

We don't get fairness by keeping within the bounds of the law; what's legal can be as unfair as what's against the law. And we do not see what is fair in the nuts and bolts of ordinary life by consulting an abstract theory of justice. In classic theory, justice is done when all of us get what is coming to us by right. But in real life there isn't always enough to go around, and we need to be fair so that some people don't get it all.

For fairness we need something that goes beyond both laws and theories. We need a sense for when things are not being done evenhandedly, when some people get too much and others get too little.

LOVE ME WELL, BUT LOVE ME FAIRLY

Do not bother romantics with fairness when they are famished for love. To worry about fairness is to be like a man dying of thirst demanding Perrier. "Fair love" is an oxymoron, like sweet salt or flat hills. We know a fair fight when we see one. And we recognize fair play when we are playing the game. But when we fall in love we fly high over the fields of fairness.

Love is an accident waiting to happen to any romantic with a careless heart. It needs no more effort than it takes a piece of dust to be swept up into a vacuum cleaner. Romantics wallow in metaphors: the right person will sit beside us and turn on a fountain to flush its crystal jets through all our spiritual arteries. A river of joy will bathe the lowlands of our being with such lush streams of pleasure that we, with our whole heart and soul, will want of all things in the world only to be swallowed in its shimmering depths. The romantic waits for love to happen the way a poor loser waits for a winning lottery ticket.

The test of reality, however, proves that we do not get lasting love by chance; we earn it the old fashioned way—by working at fairness. Romance can keep love alive for a shining season; unfair love will freeze by late fall.

We need fairness whenever we share our selves with each other. Fairness is at stake in every conversation, in every sharing of duties, in every argument, in every syllable of the communications of love. We need fairness in our trust; it isn't fair to let a person down. We need fairness in our talk; it isn't fair to use words that violate a person's feelings or betray a person's confidence. We need fairness when we divide the chores; it isn't fair to load one person with all the work it takes to keep a place the way lovers want to have it. We need fairness when we decide who goes out to work for a living and who stays home to mind the children; it isn't fair for one person to get all the gravy.

Lovers who have no bent for fairness end up hurting each other badly. We are wounded by unfairness when someone who loves us insults us in the presence of strangers. We are assaulted by unfairness when people who love us leave us in the cold while they tend to strangers. We are violated by unfairness when someone leaves us alone with only a painful memory of his broken promises. Unfair love is mean and cruel, and in the end is no love at all.

Goodness knows, fairness is not enough—even though nothing else is enough without it. Imagine a marriage where everything was done with frowning fairness, but neither person felt a touch of affection. If we could make life fair for every person in the world but lose our love in the bargain, we would eventually pound at heaven's gates and beg to have our love again.

Fairness needs love as the seed in the cold earth needs the nurture of the warming sun.

But love needs fairness as the flowing river needs its firm clay.

Love may be the heavenly vision, but fairness is the guiding light. When is love fair?

Love is fair when it builds up both the lover and the

beloved, when it increases both and diminishes neither, when it brings them close and lets them be separate, when it nourishes both and leaves neither wanting.

Fair love respects the boundaries of the other person's selfhood. It postpones its most legitimate desires to meet its loved one's needs. It declines every impulse to take advantage of a weakness. Fair love does not use ancient and forgiven wrongs against the beloved. And our love is fair when we decline any pleasure that comes at the price of another's pain.

If we wrote down all the ways of fair love, the world would not hold the books we filled.

Love me well, but love me fair, or I would rather that you love me not at all.

FLAWED LOVERS MAKE UNFAIR LOVE

Certain kinds of lovers are almost always unfair to people they love. Their love is flawed by a flaw within themselves. They really do mean to love and yet, as predictably as a leaking pen stains a linen shirt, they soil their love with unfairness. Let's look at a few flawed lovers. In them, we may see a shadow of ourselves.

The Narcissist

Narcissistic people do not see other people or feel other people; they only see and feel themselves in the mirror of other people. Another person exists only when she exists for the narcissist.

Narcissists require everyone close to them to function as a reflection in which they, the narcissists, can see themselves as lovable. Friends exist only to fill the gaping hole in their empty egos. As long as their friends approve, narcissists feel worthy. If friends find a fault, they become enemies. When loved ones fog the mirror in which narcissists must see their own worth, the loved ones are seen as betrayers. In this way narcissists hold everyone else hostage to their own aching needs.

I have watched a narcissist treat his sick and dying wife as if his dying loved one was the enemy. He could not grieve for his dying spouse; he could only grieve for his own pain at having to watch his spouse die. And yet, after the spouse died, the narcissist heaved an ocean's wave of grieving love. But he did not grieve for the lost spouse, he grieved for his own lost self.

Narcissists live on the extreme edge of a need we all share. We all see ourselves in the mirror of other people's feelings about us. The difference is that narcissists can find themselves only in that mirror. This is why they always love unfairly.

The Sentimentalist

Sentimentalists paint their world in soft hues and tranquil tones. If their world is harsh brown, they will have it a gentle mauve. If reality is a clash of cymbals, they will hear a mushy waltz.

The sentimentalist is the commandant of a Nazi concentration camp who is moved to tears when he hears a German folk song played by a ragtag orchestra of doomed Jewish prisoners who will soon die in his ovens. The sentimentalist is a mother who feels good because her daughter is doing fine, while the girl is actually on drugs and is doing badly. The sentimentalist is a believer whose religion gives him only warm and cozy feelings about the beauty of the earth, while people in his parish are perishing for want of the earth's bounty. The sentimentalist is a wife who feels the glow of trusting love, while her husband flaunts his infidelities.

Sentimentalists will not have unpleasantness or confrontation in their experience of reality; they will only have their good feelings. And when anyone shoves tough reality into the mix, they pout and whimper that people are too cruel. Sentimentalists love unfairly because they cannot be honest with reality.

The Reformer

Reforming lovers simply cannot let people be. People are never quite right the way they are. If they are a success, reformers will nag them on to triumph. If they are sinners, reformers will convert them into saints. Reforming lovers shove and pull and twist the people they love until they shape them to the lover's vision.

In the ninth grade, when Mrs. Sheridan baptized me into poetry, I memorized some lines from Henry Wadsworth Longfellow's *Hiawatha* that struck me then as a romantic image of a man's relationship with a woman:

> *As unto the bow, the string is,*
> *So unto the man is woman.*
> *Though she bends him, she obeys him,*
> *Though she draws him, yet she follows.*

My dream! A beauty of a woman leads me, draws me, bends me; and when she conquers me, she falls faithfully into my power. And if she does not follow and obey, the male must reform her. Oh, Longfellow! You bewitched me!

But women can have just as much reforming zeal as men have. "Joe is too easygoing now, but after we get married, I'll light a fire under him." "James is a saint, but the poor thing has no idea how people take advantage of him; never mind, I'm going to put some steel in his backbone." "Well, now that we're engaged, we'll have to get you some decent clothes. Look, I've already thrown out your old ties and bought you these wonderful foulards."

Reforming lovers often grumble over the people they love. "Must I forever take care of you?" But let him even hint that he might go it on his own, and she panics. "Hah, you'd make a mess of your life without me."

The Addictive Lover

Addictive lovers are most unfair to themselves.

Helen Ponstein was slavishly in love with Joseph Fragmeir. Joseph answered her self-sacrificing love by breaking her nose, knocking out her teeth, and punching her ears until she lost part of her hearing.

And yet she loved him. "I worshiped him. He was like a god to me."

Addictive lovers flow with only one current—the white water of cavernous need. Their need is so deep, so enormous, that they have nothing to give each other. Both of them hate their own emptiness. One feels a need to be punished, the other feels a need to punish; one wants pain, the other wants guilt. So they get from each other what they think they deserve.

Two empty human beings meet, each longing to be filled by the other. They are codependents, but neither has anything the other can depend on. They are addicts who can never get what they need from the other's emptiness. All they can do is keep sucking on the breast that has no milk. They will be unfair in their love until they discover that they are not really empty, that they have the power to give as well as the need to receive.

The Midlife Lover in Heat

I have known men with such sensitivity to justice that the slightest bruise suffered by poor people arouses them to a crusade against man's inhumanity to man. Yet, they are stricken blind and deaf to their own unfairness when they get into heat.

Take Kermit Onrecht. He and his wife, Selma, had

finally pushed their three children out of the nest. She had done the childrearing while he was making a success of himself in the world outside. Now it was her day, and she wanted to make something out of herself just as Kermit had. And now that it was her turn, she expected Kermit to help her.

But things were not what they used to be, not for Selma and not for Kermit.

Selma, as Kermit saw her, had gotten just a little bit lumpy, a little gray, and a little tired on the way; maybe a trifle dull. Kermit, on the other hand, was sure that he had grown beyond Selma's potential. So he began to chafe at the bit of his midlife bridle and was fretting for a chance to get some of the frothier satisfactions he still had it in him to relish.

It was then that he met Susan, she with unusual gifts for persuading middle-aged men that they had untapped energies for rhapsodic love. She worked wonders on Kermit. He was swallowed alive by love.

How right it was! How fated, how undeniable! What could a man of spirit do but surrender to passion's beauty, its goodness, and to Susan?

Selma fought back.

"It isn't fair. How could you be so unfair to me? Why can't you see how unfair you are?"

"Unfair? You talk unfair? Let me tell you what is unfair. It is unfair that I should be trapped in a marriage that has nothing in it for me. It's fair for me, finally, to get the happiness I have coming and never had with you. It's fair, Selma, it's fair. One day you'll see for yourself how fair it is."

"One day you will go to hell."

Locate any respectable person of middle age, any at all, open the primeval sluices and let the waves of erotic love flood his parched heart, and that utterly fair-minded person will die to fairness.

Nobody is free from the flaws that turn love unfair. This is why fair love comes hard for everyone. We all have a streak of the narcissist, the sentimentalist, the reformer, and the dependent in us. But some people are sold into one of these flaws. And they make life unfair for people they love.

TESTING LOVE FOR FAIRNESS
There are some practical, if imprecise, ways of knowing fair love when we see it. Here are some of them.

Fair Love Has an Eye for Critical Differences
The pink neon sign read: "Salon for Pampered Pets." I moseyed in to look around. In the back room I came on the proprietor kneeling in front of a white poodle, painting its toenails primrose pink.

I asked him about his philosophy of pet grooming. He believed, it turned out, that any pet dog deserved the same loving care that a person gets. "A guy came in here once grousing to his wife about paying good money to get the dog groomed for Christmas. So I told him what I always say to people who show no respect for pets: 'Spell *dog* backwards, mister!' "

'Spell dog backwards?'

'You bet. D-o-g backwards is g-o-d.' That got him where it really matters. Does it every time."

I allowed as it probably did. Still, it seemed to me that *dog* spelled backwards is just misspelled *dog*.

Some people do get the two confused. They love God the way they love a dog. They expect Him to come when He is called, tail wagging, ready to fetch whatever it is they want fetched. Other people love their dog the way only God should be loved. They need the comfort only God can give, as we all do, but they turn to their comfortable dog to get it.

More of us love people the way we love dogs.

What most of us want from the dog we love comes down to three things. First, we want him to know that we *own* him. Second, we want him to *obey* us. And third, we want him to *depend* on us *all* the years of his life.

Some people want the same three things from people they love. Listen to the aging lover (a François Mauriac character) talk about a young mistress he once owned: "I had to have her constantly at my beck and call. She always had to be there when I wanted her. She was my property. I ought to have been a slaveholder." Here is a woman (another Mauriac character) solacing herself after her husband had run off with another woman. "He was just like a dog I was dragging about on a lead."

And then there are loving parents who expect the offspring they love to depend on them for the rest of their lives. They do not trust their loved children to struggle, to fail, to feel pain, and in general to risk the hazards of living in an unfriendly world. How like loving a dog.

Fair love discerns the real differences between the objects of our love and loves each with a love that fits the distinct sorts of objects they are.

Fair Love Gives Lovers Some Space Between Them

We begin our life story submerged in our mother; for a time all we are, body and soul, is mother's baby. Then we move away, or we are pushed away. But we spend the rest of our lives coping with one part of us that wants to fly back to mother, or to a fantasy of what mother should have been.

We never get over the anxiety of hanging by ourselves on life's thin limb. Something in us wants to curl up inside mother's womb or father's lap again. And since we cannot go back home, we look for somebody else to hold us the way she did or he did.

But when we do get ourselves in the lap of a substitute parent, we feel smothered again, just as we felt when mother held us too long. We need to regain our individuality; we need separation again. So we move apart a pace.

Fair love allows the other to move, to be separate and distinct, and welcomes the loved one back again.

Fair love is an endless oscillation, ebb and flow, flux and reflux, seesaw marjorie daw. It holds and lets go, gives the comfort of closeness and the freedom of individuality. In fair love we move as a couple dancing the gavotte; we enter and exit, face each other and turn away, in and out, all to the rhythm of need for closeness and the need for separation.

Fair Love Keeps the Circle Open

Love creates a closed circle; there isn't room for everyone. Lovers have limits even if love does not. But fair love keeps the circle open at the right places, else love is unfair to those outside.

I think that children create the cruelest circles of all.

When our family first came to California, we enrolled our daughter Cathy in the sixth grade of a private school that had a reputation for serious teaching. She sidled into the class, alone, hoping against hope that someone would be her friend. But these children had been together since kindergarten, and they had formed circles within circles within circles, each a tight little fortress of friendly affection.

In the very center of the center circle was Noreen Platmund, daughter of Trinity Baptist's Platmunds, one of the evangelical powers in town and generous sponsor of the school. The Platmunds owned a cabin at Big Bear Lake in the San Bernardino Mountains, where they sometimes brought Noreen's less privileged friends. This spring Mrs. Platmund planned to invite all of the girls of Noreen's class to a weekend party in the mountains; they would share station wagons and head for the hills the moment the graduates were given their last benediction.

Forget all the snubs of the entire year; this weekend was for everyone.

But each day of May came and each day went and no invitation arrived for Cathy.

I think she kept a feeble hope alive that Mrs. Platmund would suddenly appear before us, take her by the hand, and say, "Why, of course, you dear child, of course you're invited, everyone is." But no such grace. The graduation ceremony expired, the female graduates grabbed their sleeping bags, brushed Cathy aside, lunged to their appointed station wagons, and headed off for Big Bear.

The five of us slunk like illegal aliens to the parking lot, bundled into our blue Plymouth wagon, and made a clean getaway. We strained to talk. I fumbled with the positive: the choir was nice. Doris wondered whether we would go camping that summer. John and Charlie tried to start a fight, but neither had the heart for a fracas. As we turned the corner into our dark street, Cathy sputtered:

"Who needs the creeps?"

But alone, in bed, Cathy hugged her brown bear and murmured a muffled protest against God and loving evangelical mothers.

"It isn't fair. It isn't fair."

Fair love reaches outside the inner circle now and then, when the time is right, to take an outsider in.

Fair Love Gives Fair Gifts

Even generous love has to be fair with its giving.

I learned this much, on a small scale, from watching Doris as she planned Christmas gifts for our three small children. To begin at the beginning, it is only fair that the gift you give one child should be more or less equal to the gift you give the others. "Equal," however, does not mean "same." The trick was to give each unique child a special gift that was right only for him or her, and yet leave none of them feeling that their parents played favorites. Fairness inside the family is a fine art.

I can still hear her, after every package had been wrapped and set under the Christmas tree: "I think we've got it right." And then comes the moral hangover: Is it fair that your kids should get so much when so many get nothing at all?

So you dig a little deeper and spread your gifts much wider. But even when you share your bounty beyond your kith and kin, you want your generosity to be fair.

Fair Love Gives the Right Things to the Right People in the Right Way.

Fair love gives the right things. Fair love gives people the things they need, not necessarily things they want. A drunk may want a drink, but what he needs is a cure. A beggar may want a handout, but what she needs is a chance to work. Charity that shoves people deeper into their impotence is unfair. Fair generosity aims at its own obsolescence.

Fair love gives the right things to the right people. Giving love has no limit. But selfless *lovers* are always limited. Nobody has an endless supply of anything. Fair love has to call its shots.

We need to know who needs our gifts most and needs them first. People who practice medicine on a battlefield know what this means. When there is not enough medicine to go around, one has to make a choice. The French gave us a word for it: *triage.* One hears it in the emergency rooms of most hospitals these days. Tough choices for tough situations. We cannot follow the tug of love alone; we need to discriminate.

Fair love gives the right things to the right people in the right way. At our house, during the Depression, coping with being poor was a sensitive vocation. We sometimes needed help, and we usually found it. But we had to hit rock bottom before my mother would ask the deacons of our church for help.

Once you took something from a deacon's helping hands you were watched by his judging eye. "We noticed that you bought a pint of strawberries at the market the other day."

"Was that a new dress your daughter wore to church last Sunday?"

"She made it herself."

"Oh really? How nice that she knows how to sew those *expensive* lace cuffs."

Giving good gifts with judgment in hot pursuit increases guilt.

Giving the right gifts in the right way increases gratitude.

Fair Love Keeps Its Commitments

Fair love dares to make commitments and cares enough to keep them.

If you are inclined to keep your bags packed so that you can move on to greener pastures whenever love's pleasures grow stale, think about this: What would life be like if the best you could ever get from anyone was, "I'll be there if it suits me, but don't count on me"?

The fact is that love without commitment leaves lovers dangling in the shifting winds of uncertainty, which is fair to nobody. Commitment creates one small island of certainty in a heaving ocean where nothing is secure. When we make a commitment to another person, we give that person a claim to a secure place on the island.

When I make a commitment to someone, I reach out into a future that neither of us can predict, and I give that someone a right to believe that one thing is predictable—my presence with her. I stretch myself into circumstances neither of us can control, and I give her the right to assume that one thing is under control—my intention to be present with her.

Fair love grows well in the soil of commitment.

Fair Love Forgives Fairly

Love has only one remedy for the unfair wounds of unfair love. The generic name for it is *forgiving*. But forgiving must be fair, or unfair mercy will make unfair pain even worse.

First of all, we must be fair to ourselves. Let us say that someone you trusted betrayed you. You want to get even; you want him to suffer as much as he made you suffer. But you can't touch him. He is too strong. Or maybe he is dead and gone. Yet the hurt he left you with lodges itself, unhealed, in your memory.

As long as you do not forgive, you are lashed to a pain you did not have coming in the first place. Now then, suppose that the only way to be fair to yourself is to forgive the person who was so unfair to you? He does not *deserve* to be forgiven. Of course not. But what do you deserve? Where is the fairness in being handcuffed to an escalator of unfair pain?

Second, we need to be fair to the people we forgive. Quick-draw forgivers are almost always unfair to the people they forgive. They spray forgiveness on us like bad breath. "Tut-tut, my dear boy, it's dreadful of you, you know, but I forgive you." They are forever getting an unfair advantage over us by the pardons we do not need.

The reason hasty forgiving can be unfair is that

forgiving always comes with blame attached; anybody who gets forgiven knows he has first been blamed.

What we often need is not to be forgiven, but to be indulged a little. Not every annoyance needs forgiveness. Some pains beg only for a little magnanimity. I need it from my wife when I switch channels mindlessly on the television set. She needs it from me when she stretches her short stories at dinner into full-length novels. With a little magnanimity, the quality of the big soul that puts up with small pains, we can reserve serious forgiving for serious offense.

Third, we must be fair to potential victims. Forgiving is not the same as tolerance. Never was meant to be. Some things are not to be tolerated. Ever. Not even when we forgive people for doing them.

A woman once called me when I was a guest on a talk show and challenged me to tell her how she could ever forgive the drunk driver who killed her four-year-old son. Another woman was listening while driving in her car. She stopped at a phone booth and called the show.

"My son, too, was killed by a drunk driver," she told us. "I hated the man. For two years I lived on the drippings of my hatred. But I awoke one night to the discovery that the man who killed my son was killing me. Inside.

"I went into counseling with a priest, who invited me to try to find healing through forgiving. I began. And I learned that forgiving is a process, a sluggish, crawling process, and it took me a long time.

"But my priest would not let me stop with forgiving. He urged me to begin a chapter of Mothers Against Drunk Driving in our town. He taught me that if I forgive a drunk driver, I must send out the word that I do not intend to tolerate drunk driving."

Fair love needs to be as intolerant of evil as it is forgiving of persons.

🌿 🌿

Love needs fairness the way a body needs a backbone. Love is soft. It needs spine to make it work well.

The heart of love needs help from the mind of fairness. Love goes out to almost anything—God, dogs, and almost all sorts of people. The mind of fairness tells us to match our loves to the sort of thing we love.

The heart beats to the rhythm of bonding; the mind of fairness signals when to let the other person go.

The heart closes the circle around the people we love most; the mind of fairness tells us to keep the circle open a notch for others.

The heart is generous; the mind of fairness tells us how to give the right gift to the right person in the right way.

The heart of love forgives people who hurt us; the mind of fairness tells the heart to forgive carefully lest it hurt people with its forgiving.

Fair love is the final mark of a pretty good person. All our personal powers lead us to fair love. The best reason for being honest, for being courageous, for being discerning, and for having self-control, is to create relationships in which people love each other fairly.

For that matter, all our personal powers are linked together in a living network. Every virtue depends on another. Without gratitude there can be no integrity; ingratitude falsifies life at the start. But integrity needs courage when honesty runs the risk of trouble. And courage needs discernment so that we can see what is going on and know when bravery calls us to act and when it calls us to stay where we are. But discernment needs self-control because when we fly off the handle we cannot see what is going on; and when we cannot see what is going on we usually end up making a mess of things. And then, at the end, all our linked powers lead us to a place where we can love each other fairly.

A pretty good person has a portion of all the powers. Each of us has them in his and her own unique blend. Some people have more of one. Other people have more of another. But the greatest of them all is love that is fair.

WHAT WILL YOU DO WITH THE LAST YEAR OF YOUR LIFE?

My brother Wes had a year of reasonably good living ahead of him, give or take a month or two—about as much as a person with a malignant tumor in his right brain could expect. But what is a person going to do with himself when he has only a year to do it?

I asked Wes, "What are you going to do with yourself?"

"I'm thinking about something, but I would feel a little silly talking about it."

"Okay, if you would rather not discuss it."

"Well, all right then, I'll tell you. What I want is to become a better person than I've been."

"A better person? But why, for goodness sake? Why do you want to worry about that at a time like this?"

"I don't know. But I would rather not talk about it anymore."

Odd thing. It wasn't at all what I expected him to say. Or what I wanted him to say.

I wanted him to sail home free on the winds of grace. I wanted him to talk about seeing sunsets. Catching the wind. A visit to Ireland. I wanted him to travel light the rest of his way, see the scenery, touch the people, hear the music. I wanted him to forget about being a good person.

Still, he made some sense.

When Pablo Casals the greatest of all cellists, was ninety years old, he still practiced the cello for four or five hours each day. Someone asked him why, at his age, he worked so hard at the fundamentals of his art. "Because," he said, "I think I am making some progress."

Life is really all about making some progress at being what we are meant to be—the way being a bud is about becoming a blossom, or being a well-born colt is about becoming a thoroughbred racer. We have an inner itch to be more of what we were meant to be, and we never know but that we are on the verge of a breakthrough.

Wes was not—few of us are—ticketed for pure sainthood. Goodness and badness will mingle in the veins of the best of us until we die. At one moment we will be more on the good side. At another moment we will feel a push toward the bad. None of us is going to get beyond our need for the grace of God and the charity of our friends. But with some help from both, we can become the sort of people who lean toward goodness. In other words, pretty good people.

Fopke's Dream

In faraway Friesland, lived a sad Frisian clerk named Fopke. He lived alone in a glum attic room with a narrow bed, a wardrobe, and one square wooden table with one straight wooden chair, in a rundown house in a shabby corner of the flat little village of Faken. Fopke was convinced that everyone in the village despised him and thought he was a ridiculous person. So he spent each night alone in his attic room dreaming of how he would do something startling one day to demonstrate that he was a person to be reckoned with.

Fopke finally decided on the one act that would prove to one and all that he was a superior person. He would kill himself. He would shoot himself in the head, for no reason except to demonstrate the great power of his will and the great courage of his heart.

Thus, on a fiercely raw afternoon of a bitter Frisian winter, Fopke purchased a cheap pistol and made plans to use it that very night. He would shoot himself in the temple while he was sitting at his table, bent slightly forward so that his head would fall on the table; his dead body would remain in its chair and keep a dignified posture.

When dusk fell he loaded his pistol with a single

bullet, set it on the table, and sat down in the chair. Then it occurred to him that his act would be more gallant in the eyes of the villagers if he were to drink a glass of Dutch gin, throw the empty glass through the window, and shoot himself as the glass flew to the street below. He stood up, poured a full glass, sat down at the table again, drank it all, and fell sound asleep.

During his deep sleep Fopke dreamed that he was carried away on the wings of the wind far beyond the earth to another world. He was gently set down in a long, luxuriant valley, much like the rolling meadows he had seen in his visits to the lowland provinces lying south of Friesland. He saw a cluster of thatched cottages in a village below him, and set out to explore the land.

In the village Fopke found human-like creatures very much like himself—except perhaps for their round and hairless heads and short legs, which appeared to have no knees and thus made their walk seem somewhat stiff. What fascinated him, however, was not what they looked like, but how they treated him and how they acted toward one another.

Whenever the creatures passed him, they would greet Fopke most cordially, bowing slightly, as if they thought him to be a very important visitor. If he happened to draw near to any of them while they were eating, they invited him to share their food—which, by the way, was flavored with spices more delicious than he had ever tasted on earth. As evening fell, people, without fail, invited him to come to their cottage and spend the night with them. He was welcomed in every village with the same trusting hospitality; though a stranger, he was treated as an honored guest.

As Fopke became more familiar with the people, he noted that they treated each other in the same trusting and generous way that they treated him. Each spoke the simple truth to the others and no one seemed to fear that any might betray him. No person ever spoke badly of another. They did not lock their doors at night against thieves. But, above all, they were loving to one another, and fair too, and totally at peace with themselves.

Fopke was terribly curious. How could these people be so good? How could they have achieved such splendid character, such peace within themselves? He began asking them questions about their goodness.

"You are all so very good. Please tell me how you all came to be good?"

"We do not know what this is, this 'good' that you speak of. We have never heard this word before."

"But surely you have heard of goodness and virtue."

"No, no, these are strange notions to us; no one has ever taught us about them. Please instruct us in these things you call virtue and goodness."

So Fopke became their teacher in matters of virtue. He began, like Socrates, to teach them what goodness was by asking questions about badness.

"What if someone were to come from another place to take your goods and live on your land?"

"Why, mercy be, if they needed it, they would be welcome to it, there is enough here for everyone."

"But how do you know they would not harm you? How do you know they would not kill your sons and rape your daughters?"

"We do not know what these words mean. What is kill and what is rape? Of these things we have never heard."

So Fopke told them stories about men and women on earth who lie and hurt each other in order to get what they desired. But his stories only bewildered the people and made them more curious. They soon talked of nothing else but badness and goodness. They babbled about it at the marketplaces. They exchanged well-considered opinions about it at dinner parties. The poets sang of it. A few of them even became professors of virtue and wrote large books about it.

As they thought and talked about good and evil, fear gradually seized their hearts. How could they be sure that their own neighbors were good people? Perhaps the good people should protect themselves from the bad people?

As their fear grew, a great change came over them. They no longer invited a stranger to share their meals or to find shelter under their roofs. They lied to each other for fear that the other would take advantage of their truth. They decided to defend themselves against the bad people by becoming bad along with them. So it was that nights in the village became dark and days were full of fear.

Fopke saw the terrible thing he had done. *He had brought about the fall.* He tempted good people to believe that thinking about goodness was the same as being good, and they fell for it. He wept for the evil thing he had done to them.

Seeing what great sorrow he had brought upon this good place, Fopke went from village to village to plead with the people.

"Listen to me," he cried, "listen to me!" I have done a terrible thing to you. But it is not too late. Stop talking about virtue. Just *be* good again. It is far, far better to be good then to talk about being good."

But the people laughed at Fopke. Now that they were learned in the ways of good and evil, they could see what a simpleminded creature he was. "Away with him! Away with him!" they cried. And they did not speak to him anymore.

❧ ❧

Fopke awoke, stiff from sitting at his table in the darkness of his attic, before morning had come to the village of Faken. He was awakened, however, to a new light within his poor soul. The new light was the truth that thinking about goodness is not the same as being good, and that it is far, far better to be good than to think about being good.

From that moment to the end of his days, Fopke determined to be a silent witness to the truth. He would not talk much about the truth he discovered in his dream. For to speak of it too much would be to deny it.

At first the people of Faken did not notice the change that had taken place in Fopke. But gradually they became aware that the sad and surly clerk who lived alone in the most dreary house in Faken had become more friendly. He even went out of his way to be helpful to them. And he always spoke with an honest but thoughtful and helpful tongue. Before long most of those with whom he lived and worked came to respect and admire Fopke; they even came to him now and then to ask his opinion of things. And whenever he believed that he truly had a truth worth sharing, he offered it to them for their consideration.

But still they wondered.

"Explain it to us," they pleaded. "Teach us how you became the good person you have become."

"Oh, my friends," he would answer, "I cannot talk about it. And please do not call me good. Only God is good. I am only on the Way. Join me if you will, but please do not ask me to speak of it."

Only rarely, and to only a few, did he ever speak of the experience that changed his life so deeply. He simply lived among the people in the growing measure of goodness that he had found. When Fopke died, the sober Frisian people of Faken buried his body in a modest grave, just north of the village at the edge of the North Sea. If you look carefully there, you will find a wind-worn marker with these scarcely readable words chiseled on its side: *Fopke fen Faken, Alles meirekkene, in ridlik goede minske,* which, translated, means: "All things considered, a pretty good person."